INTRODUCTION

This book contains ten stencil alphabets, each shown in two different sizes, that can be cut out and used again and again for lettering on paper of any weight and for decorating walls, floors, furniture, fabrics, tin, leather and almost any other surface. Represented are Roman Stencil, Futura Black, Art Nouveau Roman and Italic, Art Deco, Old English, Brushstroke, Victorian, Shadow Letter and Gothic Sans Serif. Each stencil plate is captioned to indicate alphabet name and size in inches.

All materials needed are inexpensive and easy to find in most well-stocked hardware or art-supply stores. The method is easily mastered and projects quickly completed.

LIST OF MATERIALS

- boiled linseed oil
- turpentine
- rags
- stencil knife and blades
- knife sharpener or carborundum stone
- ice pick
- straightedge
- cutting surface (*glass, wood, etc.*)
- #4 artists' brush
- masking tape
- paint
- textile paint (*for fabric*)
- stenciling brushes
- newspaper
- fine sandpaper
- desk blotters (*for fabric*)
- varnish (*for floors, wood, tin*)

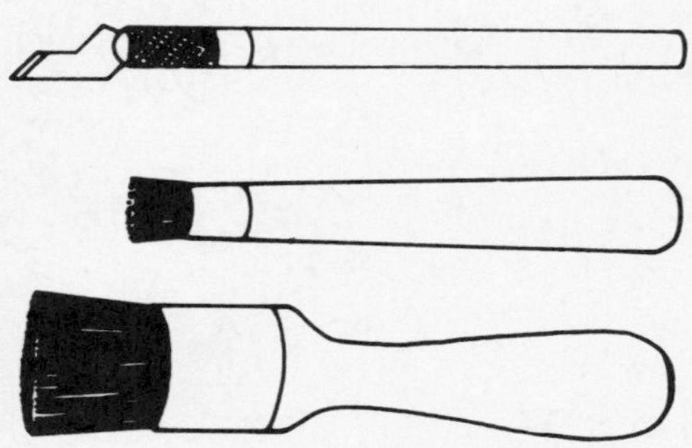

Stencil knife and two stenciling brushes of different sizes.

First, cut out an entire page (= stencil plate) from the book with a pair of scissors. The margin around the alphabet makes the stencil sturdy and durable while in use and protects the surrounding areas from paint when stenciling.

The pages of this book are of medium-weight manila paper, which must be treated with oil to make it tough, leathery and impervious to moisture. Oiled manila will become semi-translucent, allowing light to penetrate slightly. A knife blade will cut through an oiled plate more easily. The oiling process takes place after the plate (page) is cut from the book but before the blacked-in areas of the alphabet are cut out, so there will be no chance of bending or ripping delicate ties (bridge areas) when applying the oil.

A mixture of 50% *boiled* linseed oil and 50% turpentine is applied with a rag to both sides of the plate until it is thoroughly saturated. The plate is then hung to dry using a thumbtack. It will dry to touch in about 10 minutes. Any excess can be wiped off with a dry rag or the plate can be allowed to dry for a longer period. The rag should then be immersed in water until it can be incinerated or removed by regular garbage disposal service. Spontaneous combustion can occur if the rag is stored for later use.

The stencil knife is used for cutting out the small pieces through which the paint will reach the surface to be decorated. Only the solid black areas of each alphabet are cut out. Suitable cutting surfaces for this task are hard wood, a piece of plate glass with the edges taped, or a stack of old newspapers. The oiled stencil plate is placed on the cutting surface and allowed to move freely. Grasp the stencil knife as you would a pencil. Apply even pressure for the entire length of a curve or line. Frequent lifting of the knife causes jagged, uneven edges. The small details of the stencil are cut out first and larger areas last to prevent weakening the plate before cutting is completed. Sharpen the blade frequently on a carborundum stone or knife sharpener.

Cutting requires careful and accurate work. A jagged line or ragged corner will stencil exactly that way in every impression of the stencil plate.

The narrow bridges of paper between the cut-out areas in the letters are known as ties. If you accidentally cut through a tie, apply tape to both sides of the tear and replace the tape when needed. Circles and small dots are difficult to cut with a knife. Various needles can be used to punch out the guide holes below the letters. Ice picks work well. Carefully use the knife or a small piece of fine sandpaper to trim and smooth the edges.

Paints used for stenciling can be water-base or turpentine-base. Any paint used must be mixed to a fairly thick consistency. Acrylic paint is an excellent water-base paint because it is fast drying and easy to clean up. Acrylics are sold in tubes or jars and come in the right consistency for stenciling. Japan paints come in small 8-ounce cans and must be thinned slightly with turpentine. Turpentine-based paints must be allowed to dry for 24 hours. Quick-drying paint is strongly recommended for use with the alphabet stencils, since the stenciling is done one letter at a time. Both acrylic and japan paint dry to a flat finish. As soon as stenciling is completed, brushes are cleaned using water for water-base paints and turpentine for oil- or turpentine-base paints.

Stenciling on fabrics requires textile paints or inks made especially for decorating on fabric. Textile paints and inks come either water- or turpentine-soluble and are mixed thinner than regular paints. The fabric must be prewashed or drycleaned to remove any sizing and allow for shrinkage. Blotters must be used underneath the fabric to absorb excess moisture and paint. After the stenciled fabric has dried, ironing will set the textile paint or ink and make the colors permanent and washable. All these coloring mediums can be purchased at an art-supply store.

Brushes used for stenciling are cylindrical. The bristles are cut all the same length, forming a circular flat surface of bristle ends. Stencil brushes come in various sizes. A good selection of sizes would be ¼ inch in diameter, ½ inch in diameter, and 1 inch in diameter. A clean brush is used each time a new color is introduced.

To begin, draw a straight line on the surface that is to be stenciled. Position the stencil of the first letter you are using so that the line you have drawn shows through the center of the guide hole below the letter. Secure the stencil plate on two sides with masking tape. If the plate is not secure, the action of the stencil brush will cause the letter to smear. Mask the neighboring letters as well to avoid stenciling more than the letter you want.

The brush is grasped like a pencil but held perpendicular to the work surface. Dip only the flat bottom of the bristles into the paint. Do not overload the brush with paint, or it will run under the plate and ruin the design. Have several sheets of newspaper nearby for pouncing out the freshly loaded brush. Pouncing is a hammerlike movement that disperses the paint throughout the bristles. When an even speckling of paint is evident on the newspaper, the brush is ready for use. Stippling is the proper term for the rapid up-and-down motion of the brush over the stencil plate. Stippling continues until the openings in the plate are completely filled in with color.

After you have completed stenciling the first letter, pencil a small dot in the guide hole to the **right** of the letter. Remove the stencil and, after the paint has dried, line up the next letter by centering the guide hole to the **left** of the letter over the dot made from the previous one. Erase guideline when your work is completed and the last paint has dried.

As soon as stenciling with any plate is finished, the plate is wiped gently with a rag or sponge dampened with water or turpentine depending on the paint in use. This increases the life expectancy of the stencil plate by helping prevent the accumulation of paint around the edges of the design.

Colors can be lightened by the addition of white and grayed and neutralized by the addition of a small amount of the complementary color. Red and green are complements as are blue and orange, yellow and purple. The grayer the color the more faded and aged the final result. Metallic bronzing powders added to paint give the appearance of iridescence. Darker colors mixed to a thinner consistency with varnish or acrylic polymer over a light ground give the effect of translucency. Sanding the stenciled letters with fine sandpaper will make them appear worn. Stencilwork on floors, woodwork and tin should be protected with several coats of good varnish.

A more detailed and specific account of the art of stenciling is contained in *The Complete Book of Stencilcraft* (Simon & Schuster), by Joanne C. Day.

ABC

DEFG

HIJK

LMN

OPQ

Plate 1 **ROMAN STENCIL** (1″)

RSTU

VWX

YZ12

3456

7890

ROMAN STENCIL (1″)

ABCDEF

GHIJK

LMNOPQ

RSTUVW

XYZ1234

567890

Plate 3 **ROMAN STENCIL** (¾″)

ABCDEFGH

JKLMNOPQR

#7

STUVWXYZ

abcdefghijklmn

opqrstuvwxyz

1234567890

ABCDEF

GHIJKL

MNOPQR

STUVWX

YZabcd

FUTURA BLACK (1″)

efghijkl

mnopqrs

tuvwxyz

12345

67890

FUTURA BLACK (1″)

Plate 7 **ART NOUVEAU ROMAN** (1″)

a b c d e f g h

i j k l m n o p

q r s t u v w

x y z 1 2 3 4

5 6 7 8 9 0

ART NOUVEAU ROMAN (1″)

ABCDEFGHI

JKLMNOPQR

STUVWXYZ

abcdefghijklm

nopqrstuvwx

yz1234567890

ART NOUVEAU ROMAN (5/8″)

ABCDEFGHI

JKLMNOPQR

STUVWXYZ

abcdefghijklm

nopqrstuvwx

yz1234567890

ART NOUVEAU ITALIC (5/8″)

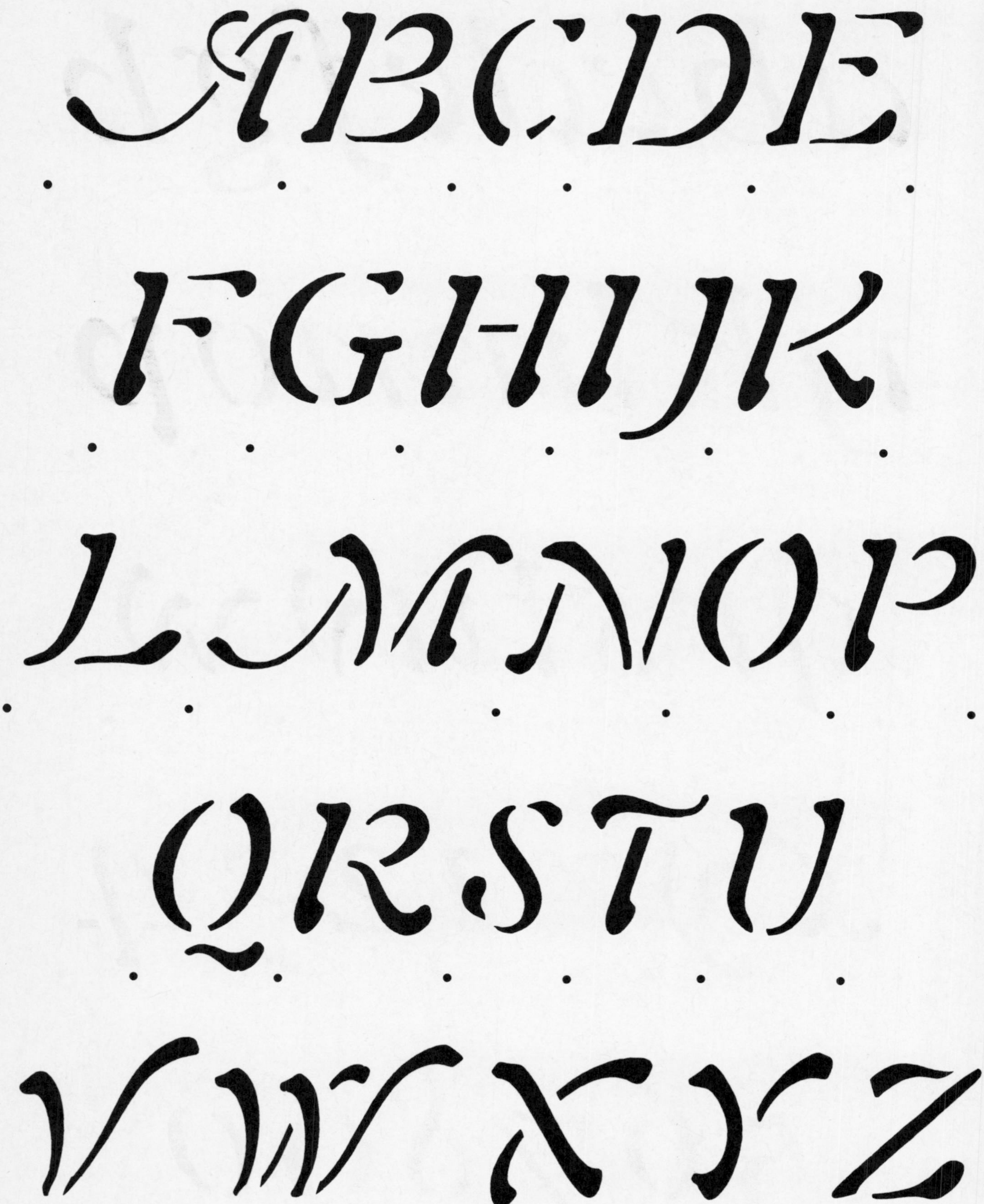

ART NOUVEAU ITALIC (1″)

abcdefgh

ijklmnop

qrstuvw

xyz1234

567890

ART NOUVEAU ITALIC (1″)

Plate 13 **ART DECO** (1½″)

ART DECO (1½″) *Plate 14*

Plate 15

ART DECO (1″)

A B C D

E F G H I J

K L M N O P

Q R S T U V

W X Y Z

OLD ENGLISH (1″)

A B C

D E F

G H I J

K L M

Plate 17 **OLD ENGLISH** (1½″)

OLD ENGLISH (1½″) ***Plate 18***

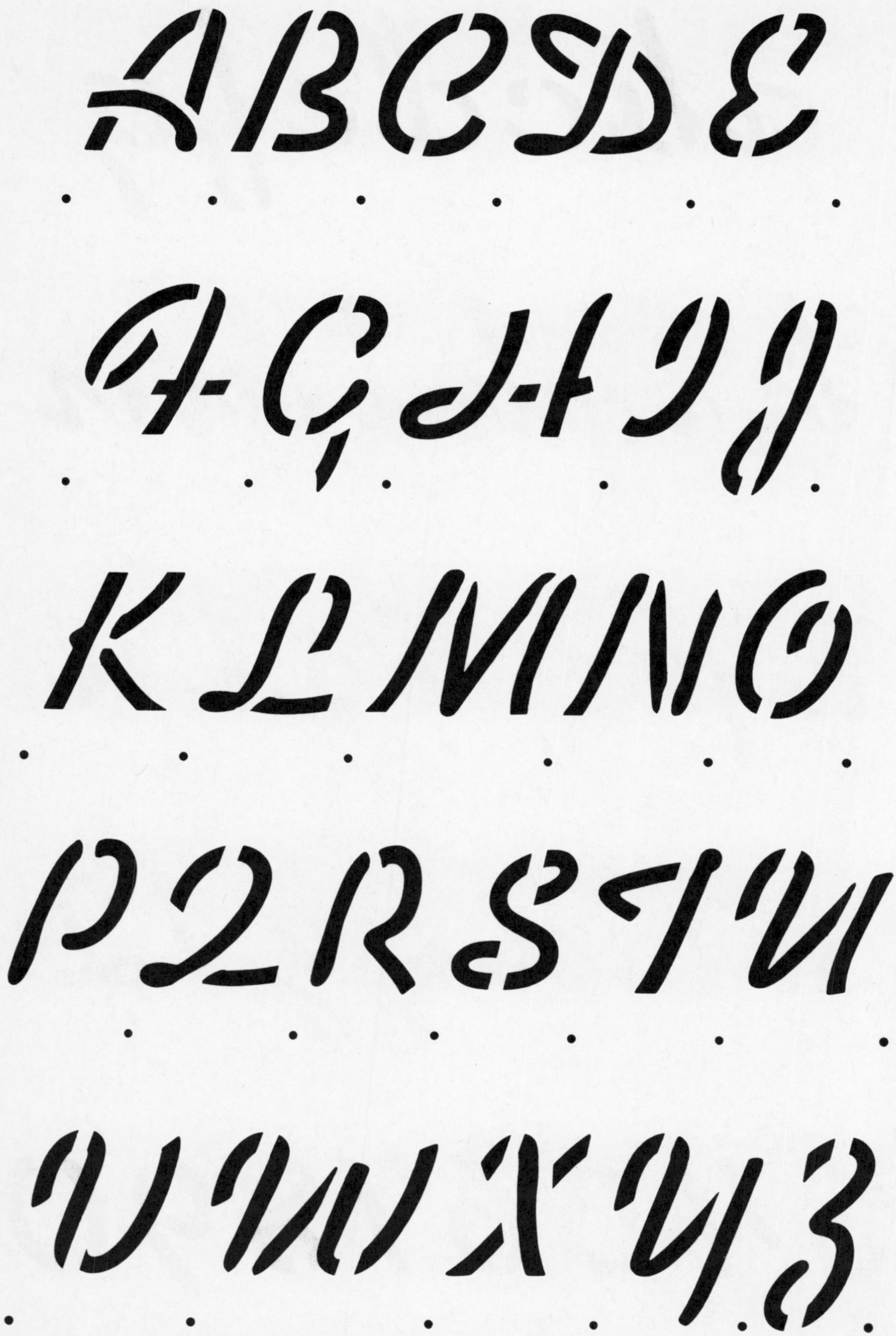

Plate 19 **BRUSHSTROKE** (1″)

abcdefg

hijklmn

opqrstu

vwxyz12

34567890

BRUSHSTROKE (1″)

ABCDEFGH

IJKLMNOPQ

RSTUVWXYZ

abcdefghijklm

nopqrstuvwx

yz1234567890

BRUSHSTROKE (11⁄16″)

#9

A B C D E F G H

I J K L M N O P Q

R S T U V W X Y Z

a b c d e f g h i j k l m

n o p q r s t u v w x

y z 1 2 3 4 5 6 7 8 9 0

VICTORIAN (3/4")

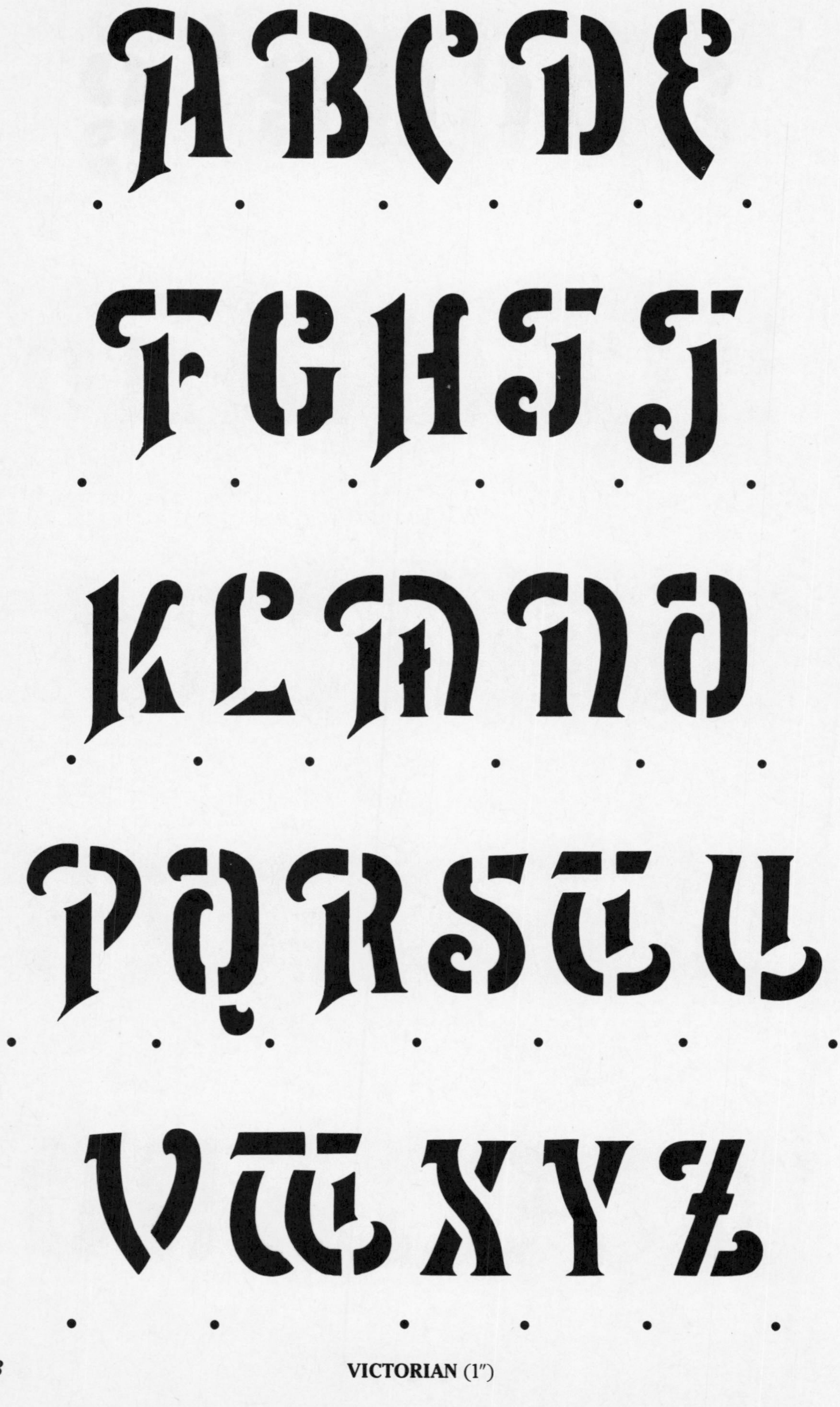
ABCDE
FGHIJ
KLMNO
PQRSTU
VWXYZ

 VICTORIAN (1″)

a b c d e f g

h i j k l m n o

p q r s t u v

w x y z 1 2 3

4 5 6 7 8 9 0

Plate 25

SHADOW LETTER (1½″)

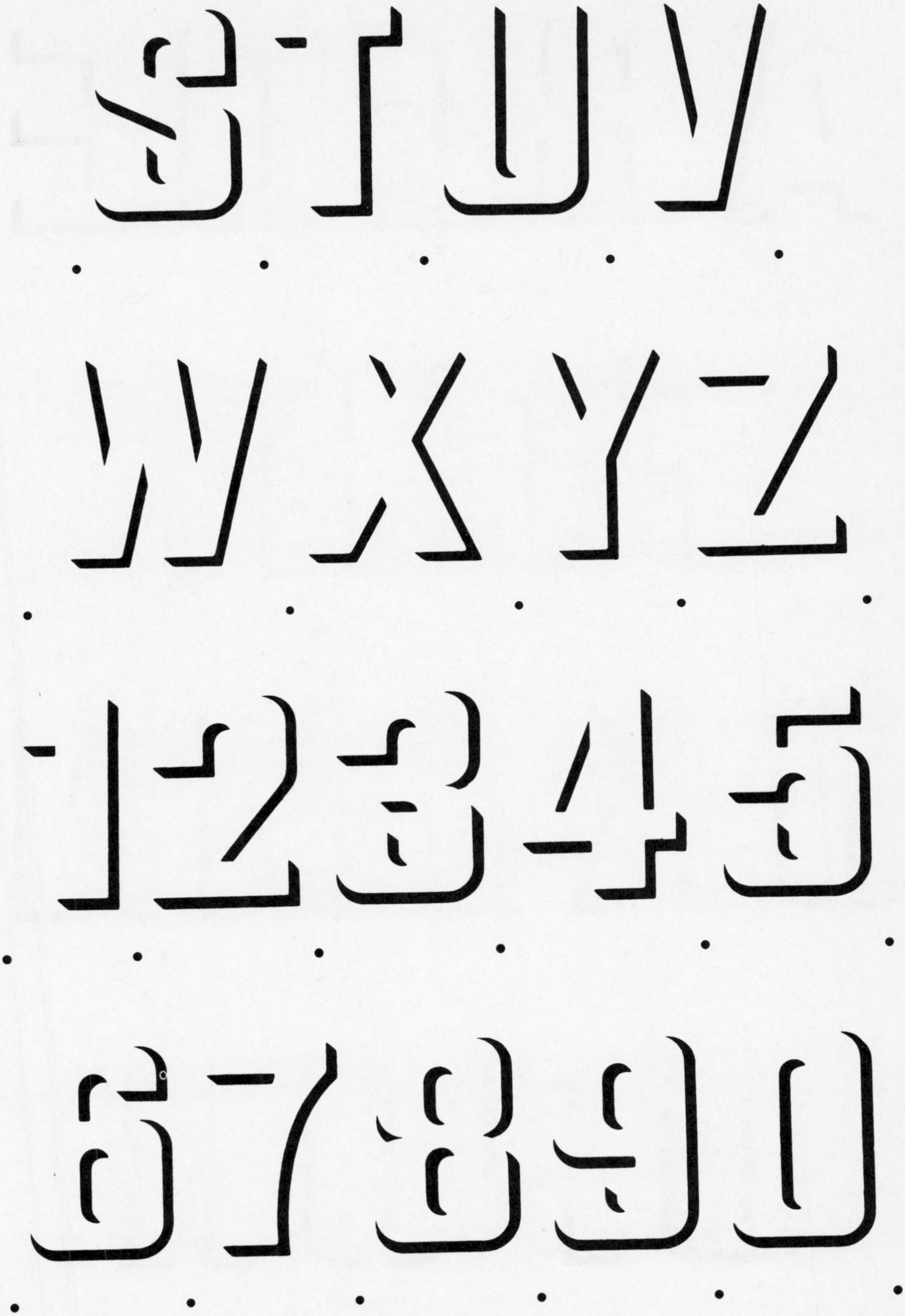

SHADOW LETTER (1½″)

ABCDEF

GHIJKLMN

OPQRSTUV

WXYZ123

4567890

Plate 27 **SHADOW LETTER** (1″)

ABCDEF

GHIJKLMN

OPQRSTUV

WXYZ123

4567890

GOTHIC SANS SERIF (1″)

ABCDE

FGHI

JKLMN

OPQR

Plate 29 **GOTHIC SANS SERIF** (1½″)

STUV

WXYZ

12345

67890

GOTHIC SANS SERIF (1½″)

CONTENTS

GRADE 6

1 Operations with Whole Numbers

WORDS TO LEARN

Place value – the position of a number showing how much it is worth
362 849 = 300 000 + 60 000 + 2000 + 800 + 40 + 9

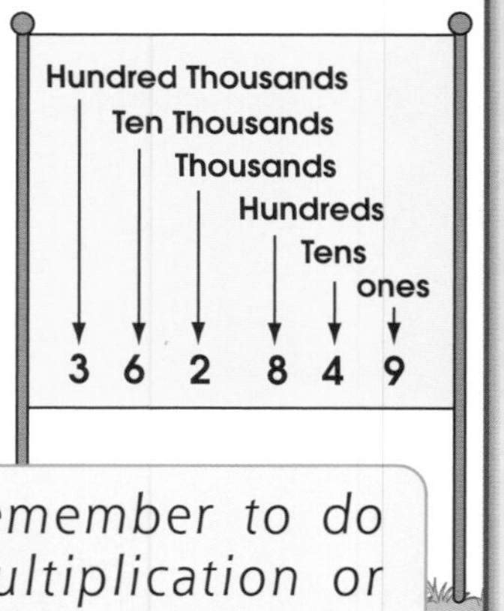

Order of operation – the operations must be done in the following order:

- Do multiplication or division from left to right.
- Do addition or subtraction from left to right.

e.g.

17 + 25 x 2	17 + 25 x 2
= 42 x 2	= 17 + 50
= 84 ✗	= 67 ✔

Look at each number. Fill in the blanks and write each number in expanded form.

① 3 is in the ______________ column; it means __________ .

Expanded form: ______________________________ .

② 6 is in the ______________ column; it means __________ .

Expanded form: ______________________________ .

③ 2 is in the ______________ column; it means __________ .

Expanded form: ______________________________ .

Put '>' or '<' in the circles.

④ 631 068 ◯ 633 860

⑤ 605 328 ◯ 650 328

⑥ 134 165 ◯ 134 516

⑦ 864 173 ◯ 846 173

⑧ 276 003 ◯ 267 300

⑨ 509 619 ◯ 510 691

Write the numbers.

⑩ 10 thousand greater than 956 430 ____________

⑪ 100 thousand less than 654 739 ____________

⑫ 100 thousand greater than 504 762 ____________

⑬ 10 thousand less than 790 653 ____________

Find the answers.

⑭ $\begin{array}{r} 121 \\ 410 \\ 213 \\ +\ 105 \\ \hline \end{array}$

⑮ $\begin{array}{r} 232 \\ 528 \\ 379 \\ +\ 110 \\ \hline \end{array}$

⑯ $\begin{array}{r} 1425 \\ 1237 \\ 422 \\ +\ 679 \\ \hline \end{array}$

When you add or subtract numbers, remember to align the numbers to the right.

⑰ $\begin{array}{r} 36284 \\ -\ 2175 \\ \hline \end{array}$

⑱ $\begin{array}{r} 40159 \\ -\ 1097 \\ \hline \end{array}$

⑲ 38 017 – 1784 = __________

⑳ 3647 + 825 + 163 + 249 = __________

㉑ 20 011 – 5200 = __________

㉒ 768 + 2593 + 1642 + 96 = __________

Estimate the answer by rounding each number to the nearest thousand. Then find the exact answer.

㉓ 892 + 916 + 1094 + 1103 = __________

Estimate ____________________

㉔ 2798 + 552 + 1211 + 3079 = __________

Estimate ____________________

㉕ 37 603 – 8343 = __________

Estimate ____________________

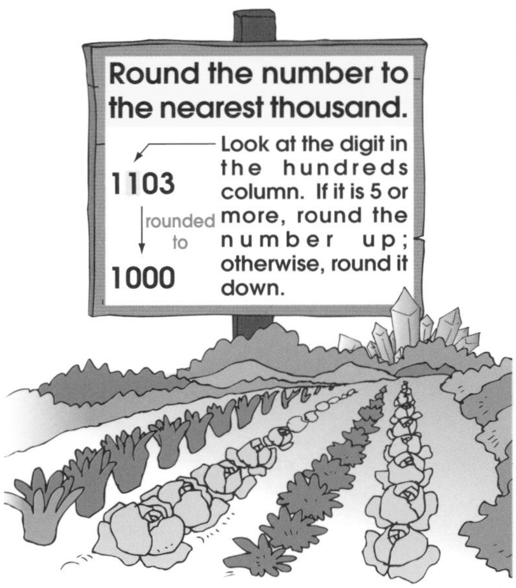

Round the number to the nearest thousand.
1103
rounded to
1000
Look at the digit in the hundreds column. If it is 5 or more, round the number up; otherwise, round it down.

Mr. Morgan, the toy factory owner, is finding out the total number of cars in the boxes. Help him find the products.

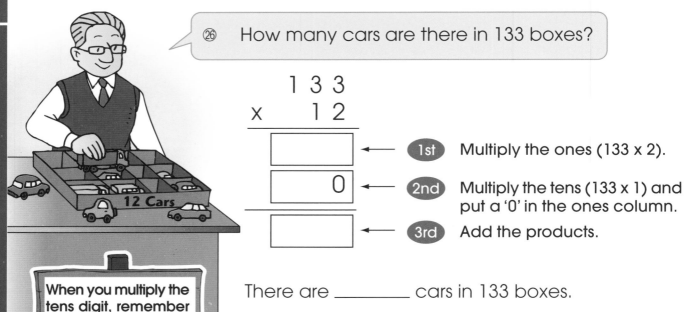

㉖ How many cars are there in 133 boxes?

```
    1 3 3
x     1 2
---------
[       ]  ← 1st  Multiply the ones (133 x 2).
[      0]  ← 2nd  Multiply the tens (133 x 1) and put a '0' in the ones column.
---------
[       ]  ← 3rd  Add the products.
```

There are ________ cars in 133 boxes.

㉗ 124×39

㉘ 768×25

㉙ 981×47

㉚ 605 x 34 = __________ ㉛ 516 x 88 = __________

㉜ 327 x 59 = __________ ㉝ 104 x 63 = __________

Estimate the answer by rounding each number to the nearest ten. Then find the exact answer.

㉞ 439 x 27 = __________

Estimate __________________

㉟ 771 x 52 = __________

Estimate __________________

㊱ 617 x 45 = __________

Estimate __________________

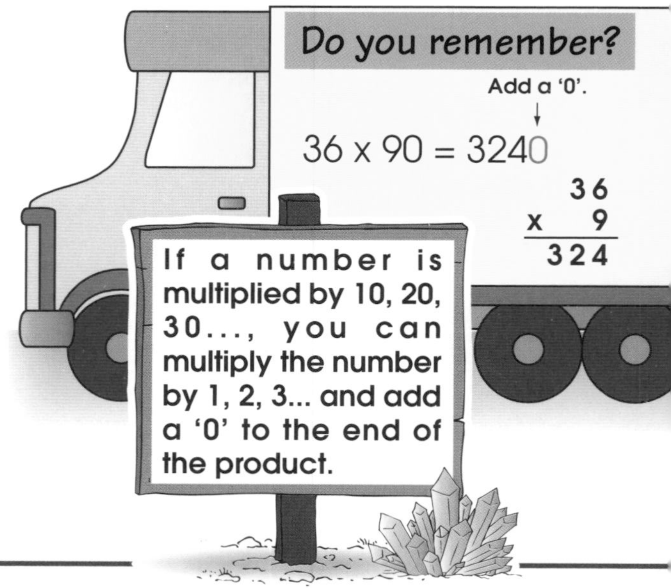

Do you remember?
Add a '0'.
36 x 90 = 3240
36
x 9
324
If a number is multiplied by 10, 20, 30..., you can multiply the number by 1, 2, 3... and add a '0' to the end of the product.

Read what Fiona the Cat says. Help her solve the problem. Then do the division.

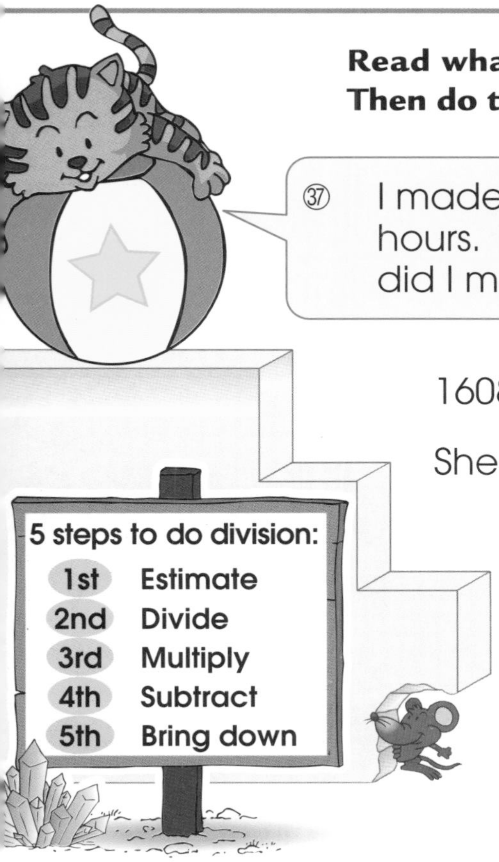

5 steps to do division:
1st Estimate
2nd Divide
3rd Multiply
4th Subtract
5th Bring down

37. I made 1608 revolutions in 12 hours. How many revolutions did I make in 1 hour?

1608 ÷ 12 = ______

She made ______ revolutions.

```
       1 ☐ ☐
   ┌────────
12 ) 1 6 0 8
     ☐☐        ↓ bring down
     ────
       4 0       bring down
       3 6           ↓
     ──────
         ☐ 8
         ☐☐
       ─────
```

38. 46) 4692

39. 39) 1599

40. 25) 8467 R

41. 18) 2953 R

42. 23) 6700 R

43. 3591 ÷ 19 = ______

44. 4026 ÷ 17 = ______

45. 4815 ÷ 35 = ______

46. 6912 ÷ 72 = ______

Use multiplication to check each division. Put a check mark ✔ in the box if it is correct; otherwise, write the correct answer.

47. 4400 ÷ 36 = 125 ☐

Check ______

48. 5184 ÷ 24 = 216 ☐

Check ______

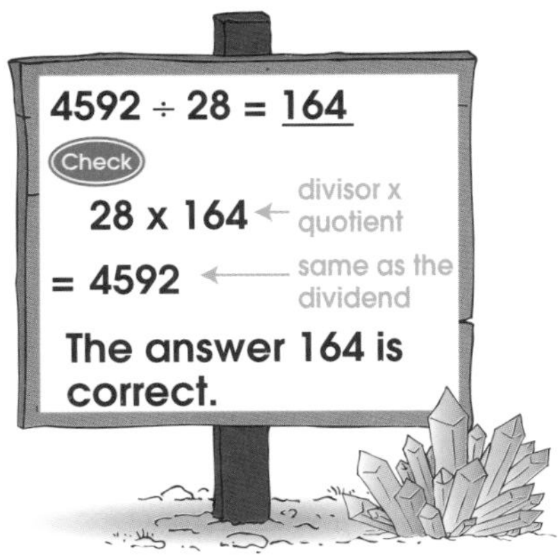

4592 ÷ 28 = 164

28 x 164 ← divisor x quotient
= 4592 ← same as the dividend
The answer 164 is correct.

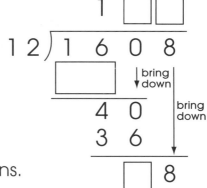

There is a concert this evening. Help the children solve the problems.

We practised 1080 min last week.

49 How many hours did the children practise last week?

__________ hours

50 The concert hall is divided into 4 sections. The seats in these 4 sections are 452, 386, 415, and 339 respectively. How many seats are there in the concert hall in all?

__________ seats

51 Each children's ticket costs $11. If 678 children attend the concert tonight, how much will be collected from selling children's tickets?

$ __________

52 If all the tickets for the concert are sold out, how many adults are there in all?

__________ adults

53 Each adult ticket costs $25. How much is collected from selling adult tickets?

$ __________

54 How much more is collected from selling adult tickets than selling children's tickets?

$ __________

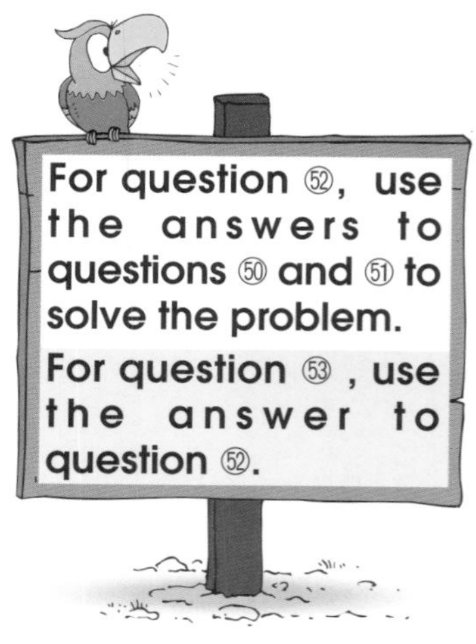

For question 52, use the answers to questions 50 and 51 to solve the problem.
For question 53 , use the answer to question 52.

Find the answers.

(55) 14 + 21 x 2

= ______ + ______

= __________

(56) 36 ÷ 3 – 11

= ______ – ______

= __________

(57) 83 – 72 ÷ 9

= ______ – ______

= __________

(58) 69 + 50 ÷ 5

= ______________

= __________

(59) 91 – 4 x 17

= ______________

= __________

See what the children are going to buy. Help them solve the problems.

Do 'x' or '÷' first.
Then do '+' or '–'.
e.g. 3 + 8 ÷ 2
= 3 + 4
= 7
Do first.
$3 each
28¢ each

(60) Mike buys 3 bread rolls. If he pays with 90¢, what is the change?

The change is __________ ¢.

(61) After buying 4 French loaves, Jason has $19 left. How much did Jason have at first?

Jason had $ __________ at first.

ACTIVITY

Look at the doughnuts in the box. Solve the problem.

The cost of the first 4 doughnuts is $3. For the remainder, each doughnut costs 50¢. How much does the box of doughnuts cost?

$ __________

2 Brackets

WORDS TO LEARN

Brackets (( )) – signs to show which part of a problem is to be done first

e.g. 5 x (2 + 4) = 5 x 6
= 30

Solve the problem inside the ( ) first.

Brackets must be used in pairs.

Read what Mrs. Martin and Janet say. Help them solve the problems.

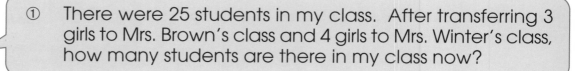

① There were 25 students in my class. After transferring 3 girls to Mrs. Brown's class and 4 girls to Mrs. Winter's class, how many students are there in my class now?

25 – (3 + _____) = 25 – _____

= _____

There are _____ students in Mrs. Martin's class now.

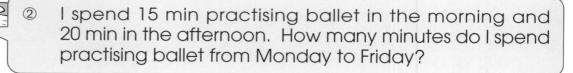

② I spend 15 min practising ballet in the morning and 20 min in the afternoon. How many minutes do I spend practising ballet from Monday to Friday?

(15 + _____) x 5 = _____ x 5

= _____

Janet spends _____ min practising ballet from Monday to Friday.

Find the answers.

③ (11 + 6) – 4
= _____
= _____

④ 4 x (16 – 9)
= _____
= _____

⑤ (42 + 6) ÷ 3
= _____
= _____

⑥ 14 + (41 – 27)
= _____
= _____

⑦ (83 – 7) ÷ 2
= _____
= _____

⑧ (15 + 5) x 8
= _____
= _____

Place brackets in each number sentence to make it true.

⑨ 99 + 33 ÷ 11 = <u>102</u>

⑩ 108 – 3 x 9 = <u>945</u>

⑪ 14 x 7 + 6 = <u>182</u>

⑫ 256 ÷ 16 – 8 = <u>32</u>

⑬ 100 – 36 ÷ 4 = <u>91</u>

⑭ 39 + 2 x 17 = <u>73</u>

Fill in the blanks.

Property of multiplication
It is like a rainbow.
2 x (18 + 27)
= 2 x 18 + 2 x 27
= 36 + 54
= 90

⑮ 7 x (3 + 5)

= 7 x ______ + 7 x ______

= ______ + ______

= ______

⑯ 4 x (18 – 7)

= 4 x ______ – 4 x ______

= ______ – ______

= ______

⑰ (31 – 15) x 9

= ______ x 9 – ______ x 9

= ______ – ______

= ______

⑱ (50 + 2) x 5

= ______ x 5 + ______ x 5

= ______ + ______

= ______

ACTIVITY

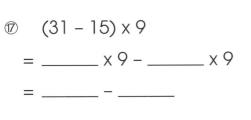

See how the children can find the answers in a faster way. Follow their method to solve the problems.

Think:
82 = 80 + 2
4 x 82
= 4 x (80 + 2)
= 4 x 80 + 4 x 2
= 320 + 8
= 328
Think:
99 = 100 – 1
5 x 99
= 5 x (100 – 1)
= 5 x 100 – 5 x 1
= 500 – 5
= 495

① 6 x 91 = __________ (Think: 91= 90 + 1)

② 9 x 59 = __________ (Think:)

③ 8 x 68 = __________ (Think:)

④ 7 x 42 = __________ (Think:)

⑤ 5 x 83 = __________ (Think:)

3 Integers

WORDS TO LEARN

Integers – zero and all whole numbers
e.g. 20, -3, 0, 15, -1, ...

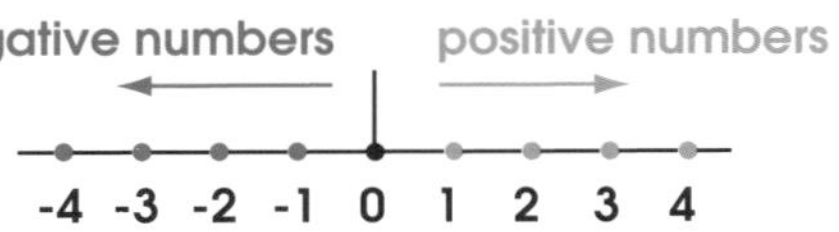

-3 and 3 are both 3 units from 0;
-3 and 3 are opposites.

The temperature is 20 °C below zero. It is -20 °C.

0, 5, -2, 3, -6... are integers.
4 units
4 units
-4 -3 -2 -1 0 1 2 3 4
-4 and 4 are opposites.

Colour the snowballs with integers.

① 12 1.4 -3 0 $\frac{2}{7}$ $1\frac{1}{6}$

1.7 8 156 -8 10.01 20

Write the opposite of each integer.

② +6 ______ ③ -15 ______ ④ -36 ______

⑤ +14 ______ ⑥ -9 ______ ⑦ +87 ______

Put '>' or '<' in the circles.

⑧ 4 ◯ -2 ⑨ -8 ◯ -7 ⑩ -14 ◯ 2

⑪ 2 ◯ 0 ⑫ 1 ◯ -11 ⑬ -7 ◯ -6

Any integer is greater than those to its left.
-4 -3 -2 -1 0 1 2
e.g. -4 < -2, 0 < 1

Write the numbers in order from smallest to greatest.

⑭ -3 -6 5 0 2 ______________________

⑮ 5 -4 3 7 1 ______________________

⑯ 1 0 -5 6 -3 ______________________

Write the temperature of each city. Then answer the questions.

⑰

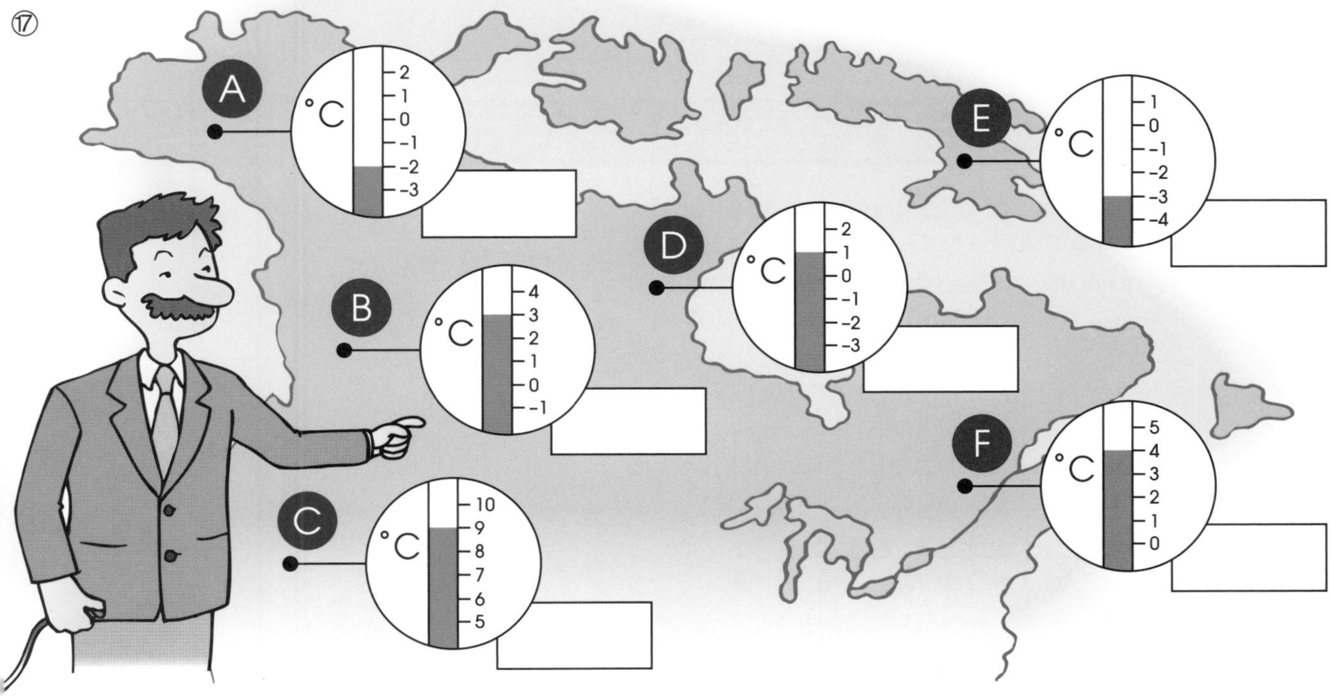

⑱ Which city has the highest temperature? ______

⑲ How many cities have temperatures below 0°C? ______

⑳ How many cities have temperatures above 0°C? ______

㉑ Which city has a temperature 8°C higher than that of D ? ______

㉒ Put the cities in order. Start with the lowest temperature.

____

ACTIVITY

Fill in the missing integers with the help of the number line.

①	-5	-3	☐	1	3	☐
②	4	2	☐	-2	☐	-6
③	3	0	-3	☐	☐	-12

4 Multiples and Factors

WORDS TO LEARN

Multiple – the product of a given number and a whole number

Common multiple – a number that is the multiple of more than one number

Multiples of 3: 3, 6, 9, 12, 15, 18, 21, 24,...
Multiples of 4: 4, 8, 12, 16, 20, 24,...
Common multiples of 3 and 4: 12, 24,...

The least common multiple (L.C.M.) of 3 and 4 is 12.

Factor – whole number that can be multiplied to get a product

The factors of 12: 1, 2, 3, 4, 6, 12
The factors of 18: 1, 2, 3, 6, 9, 18

Common factors of 12 and 18: 1, 2, 3, 6

The greatest common factor (G.C.F.) of 12 and 18 is 6.

Which cans should Teddy aim for? Write the numbers.

① Teddy wants to throw the balls into every 2nd can.

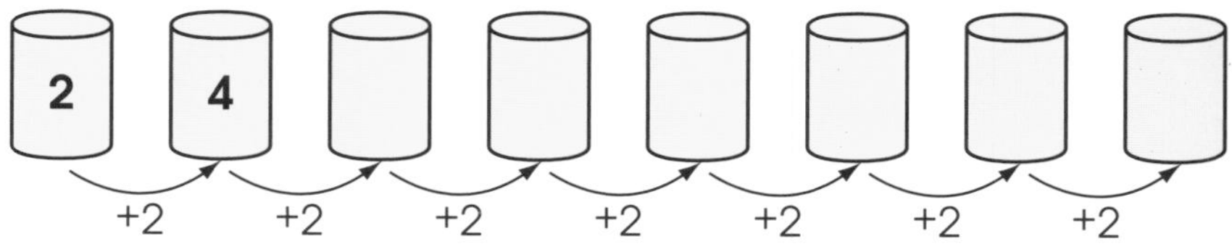

② Teddy wants to throw the balls into every 3rd can.

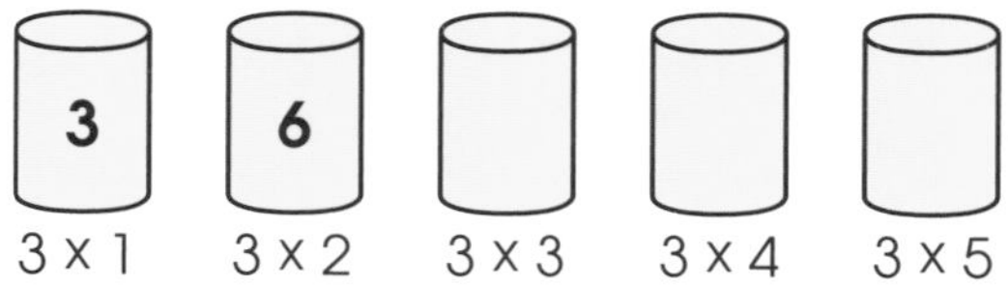

Write the first six multiples of each number.

③ 5 : ______ , ______ , ______ , ______ , ______ , ______

④ 7 : ______ , ______ , ______ , ______ , ______ , ______

⑤ 9 : ______ , ______ , ______ , ______ , ______ , ______

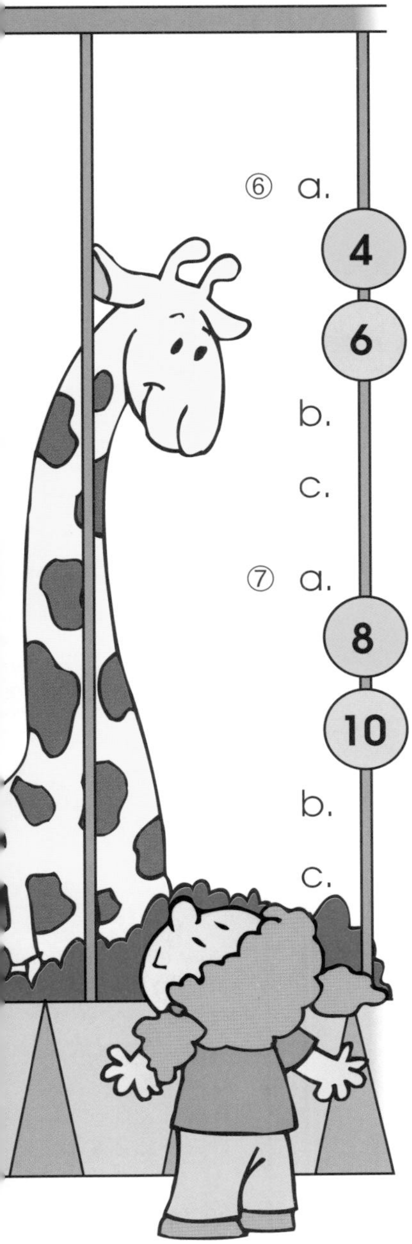

Find the first eight multiples of each number. Then write the common multiple(s) and the L.C.M. of each pair of numbers.

⑥ a.

4 : ____ , ____ , ____ , ____ , ____ , ____ , ____ , ____

6 : ____ , ____ , ____ , ____ , ____ , ____ , ____ , ____

b. Common multiples of 4 and 6: ____ , ____

c. The L.C.M. of 4 and 6: ____

⑦ a.

8 : ____ , ____ , ____ , ____ , ____ , ____ , ____ , ____

10 : ____ , ____ , ____ , ____ , ____ , ____ , ____ , ____

b. Common multiple of 8 and 10: ____

c. The L.C.M. of 8 and 10: ____

List the multiples of each number. The first common multiple is their L.C.M.

Write the first four common multiples of the numbers. Then find the L.C.M.

⑧ 4 5 Common multiples: ____________

L.C.M.: ______

⑨ 3 9 Common multiples: ____________

L.C.M.: ______

⑩ 2 6 Common multiples: ____________

L.C.M.: ______

How many different columns can Louis build with 14 blocks? Write the numbers.

All the columns should have the same number of blocks.

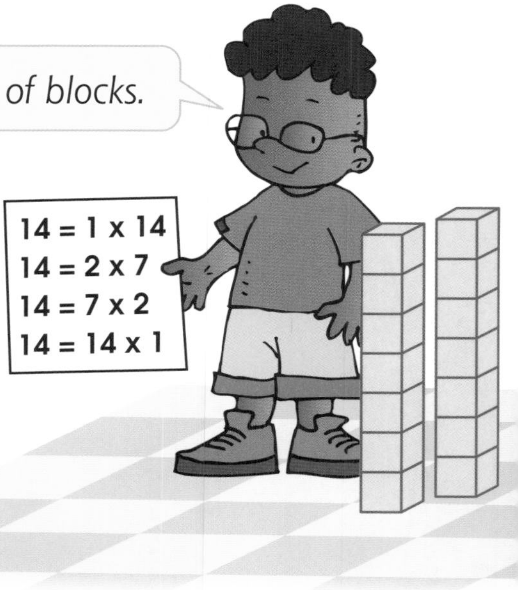

⑪ 1 column of blocks: each column has ______ block(s).

⑫ 2 columns of blocks: each column has ______ block(s).

⑬ 7 columns of blocks: each column has ______ block(s).

⑭ 14 columns of blocks: each column has ______ block(s).

⑮ The factors of 14 are ______ , ______ , ______ , and ______.

Stop when you get to a number you've already come across.
e.g. 6 = 1 x 6
6 = 2 x 3
6 = 3 x 2
Stop here!

Find the factors of each number.

⑯ 12 = 1 x ________

12 = 2 x ________

12 = 3 x ________

The factors of 12 are:

____

⑰ 20 = 1 x ________

20 = 2 x ________

20 = 4 x ________

The factors of 20 are:

____

⑱ The factors of 24 are: ______________________________

⑲ The factors of 30 are: ______________________________

⑳ The factors of 32 are: ______________________________

㉑ The factors of 36 are: ______________________________

㉒ The factors of 40 are: ______________________________

Find the factors of each number. Then write the common factors and G.C.F.

23. a. **20** : ______ , ______ , ______ , ______ , ______ , ______

    28 : ______ , ______ , ______ , ______ , ______ , ______

    b. Common factors of 20 and 28: ______ , ______ , ______

    c. G.C.F. of 20 and 28: ______

24. a. **25** : ______ , ______ , ______

    45 : ______ , ______ , ______ , ______ , ______ , ______

    b. Common factors of 25 and 45: ______ , ______

    c. G.C.F. of 25 and 45: ______

Find the common factors and G.C.F.

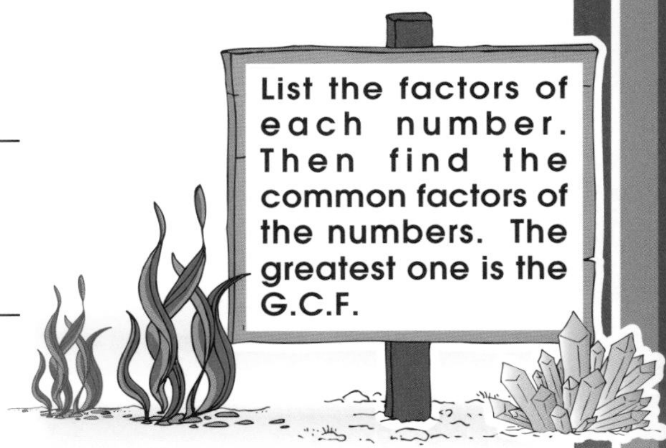

List the factors of each number. Then find the common factors of the numbers. The greatest one is the G.C.F.

25. 30, 35 Common factors: ____________

    G.C.F: ________

26. 48, 56 Common factors: ____________

    G.C.F: ________

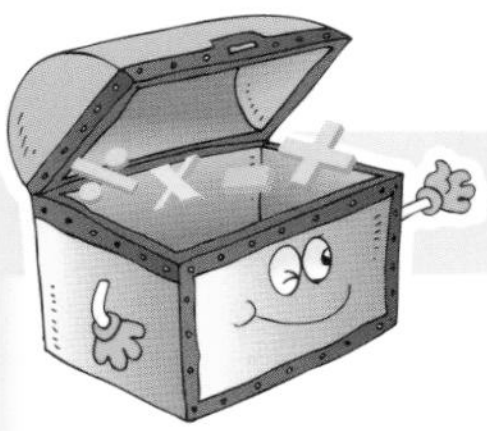

ACTIVITY

Help Freddie the Fish solve the problem.

I want to make friends with 24 shrimps and 30 crabs. How many days would it take me to do that if I meet the same number of shrimps and the same number of crabs each day?

It would take ________ days. Freddie the Fish has to meet ________ shrimps and ________ crabs each day.

5 Composite and Prime Numbers

WORDS TO LEARN

Composite number – any number greater than 1 that has more than 2 factors
Prime number – any number with only 1 and itself as factors

8 has 4 factors. They are 1, 2, 4, and 8. 8 is a composite number.
8
8 is a composite number.
8 is a prime number.

Help the children find the number of stickers in each group and write 'composite' or 'prime'.

If the number can form a rectangle, it is a composite number.
e.g. 10
10 is a composite number.

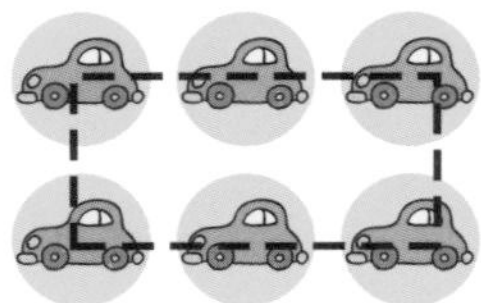

6 = 2 x 3 ; 6 can form a rectangle.
6 is a composite number.

① 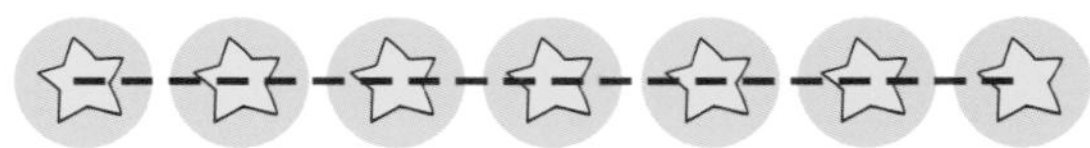

____ = 1 x 7 ; 7 is a ______________ number.

② 

____ = 1 x 5 ; 5 is a ______________ number.

③ 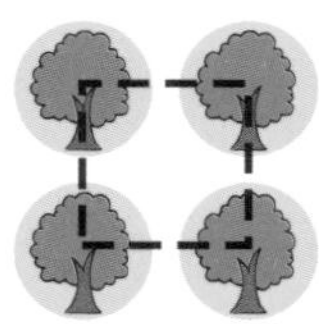

____ = 2 x 2 ;
4 is a ______________ number.

Write 'prime' or 'composite' for each number.

④ 21 ______________ ⑤ 19 ______________ ⑥ 30 ______________

⑦ 43 ______________ ⑧ 65 ______________ ⑨ 74 ______________

Follow the children's way to write each number as a product of prime factors.

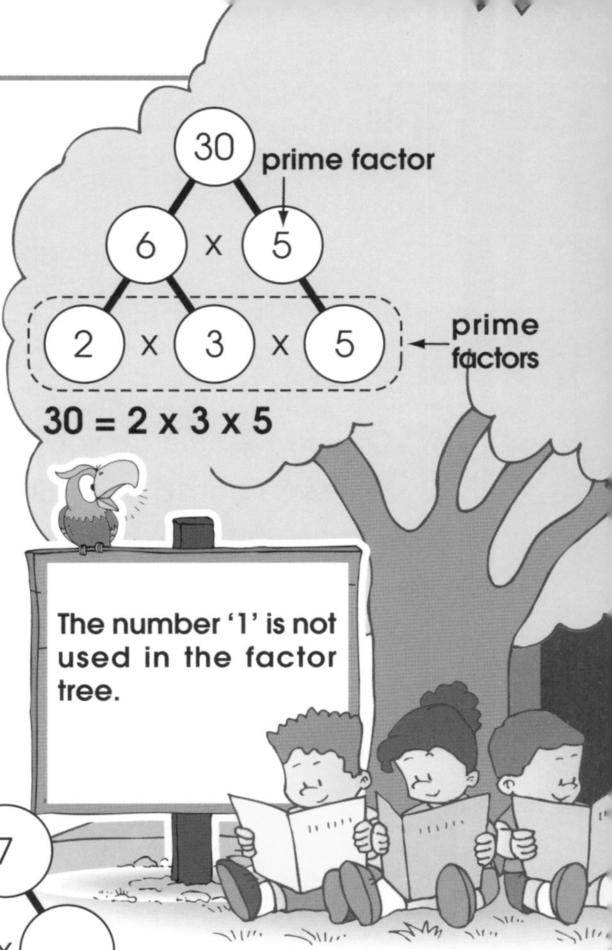

Steps to write numbers as a product of prime factors:

- **1st** Write the composite number as the product of two factors.
- **2nd** Continue to factorize each composite number until all factors are prime numbers.
- **3rd** Write the number as a product of prime factors.

⑩

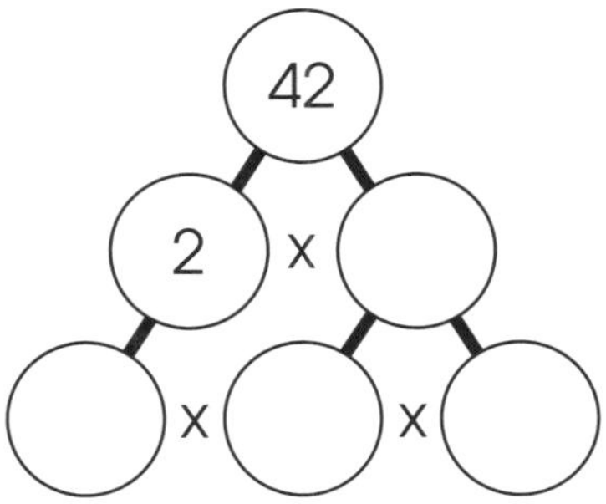

42 = ____________________

⑪

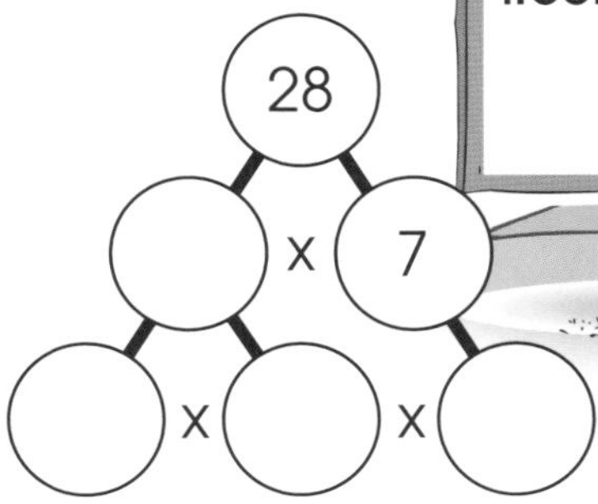

28 = ____________________

⑫

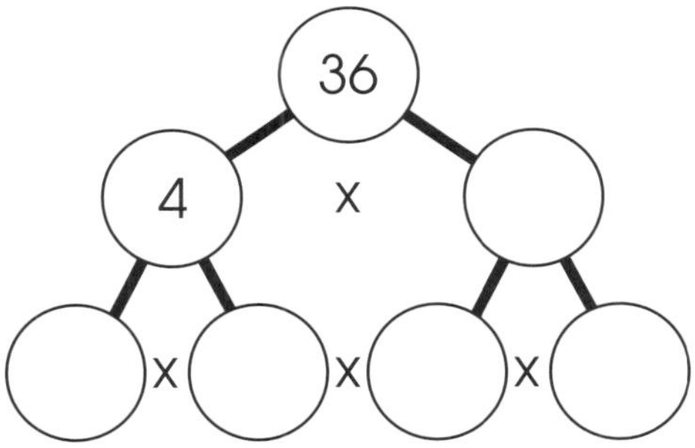

36 = ____________________

⑬

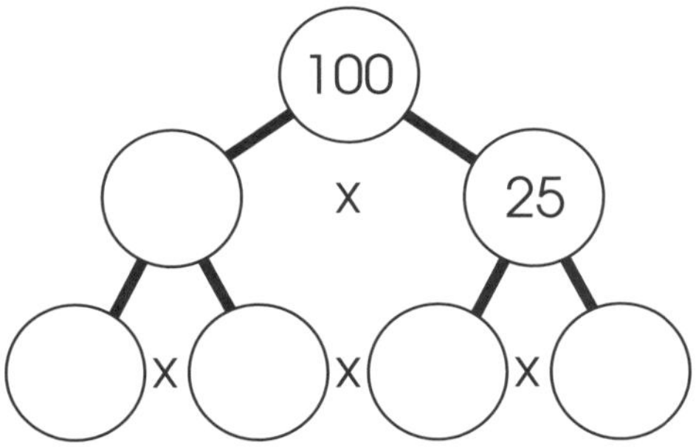

100 = ____________________

⑭ 66 = ____________________

⑮ 52 = ____________________

⑯ 74 = ____________________

⑰ 96 = ____________________

⑱ 81 = ____________________

⑲ 88 = ____________________

⑳ 32 = ____________________

㉑ 40 = ____________________

㉒ 24 = ____________________

㉓ 58 = ____________________

5

Follow Matthew's method to find the greatest common factor (G.C.F.) of each pair of numbers.

Find the G.C.F. of 16 and 20.

16 = 2 x 2 x 2 x 2

20 = 2 x 2 x 5

Common prime factors: 2, 2

The G.C.F. of 16 and 20: 2 x 2 = 4

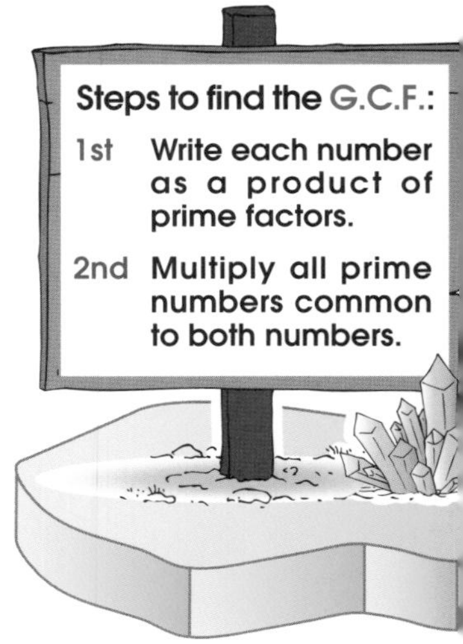

Steps to find the G.C.F.:
1st Write each number as a product of prime factors.
2nd Multiply all prime numbers common to both numbers.

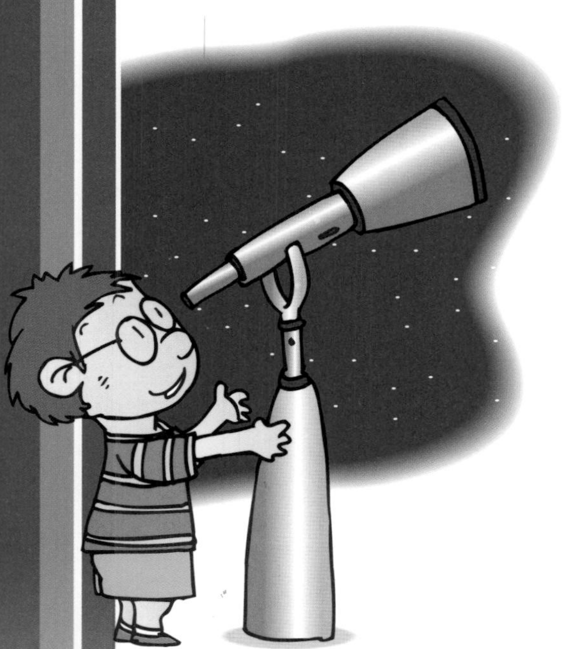

㉔ **30** = ____ x ____ x ____

45 = ____ x ____ x ____

Common prime factors: ____ , ____

G.C.F.: ____ x ____ = ________

㉕ **48** = ____ x ____ x ____ x ____ x ____

72 = ____ x ____ x ____ x ____ x ____

Common prime factors: ____ , ____ , ____ , ____

G.C.F.: ____ x ____ x ____ x ____ = ________

Write each number as a product of prime factors. Then find the G.C.F.

㉖ **12** = ____________________

20 = ____________________

G.C.F.: ________

㉗ **15** = ____________________

60 = ____________________

G.C.F.: ________

㉘ **8** = ____________________

40 = ____________________

G.C.F.: ________

㉙ **56** = ____________________

64 = ____________________

G.C.F.: ________

Follow the alien to find the least common multiple (L.C.M.) of each pair of numbers.

Steps to find the L.C.M.:
1st Write each number as a product of prime factors.
2nd Sort out the common prime factors and multiply them to all other factors.

Find the L.C.M. of 16 and 20.

16 = 2 x 2 x 2 x 2

20 = 2 x 2 x 5

L.C.M.: 2 x 2 x 2 x 2 x 5 = 80

㉚ **10** = ____ x ____

66 = ____ x ____ x ____

L.C.M.: ____ x ____ x ____ x ____

= ________

㉛ **35** = ____ x 7

50 = ____ x ____ x ____

L.C.M.: ____ x ____ x ____ x ____

= ________

㉜ **15** = ____ x ____

21 = ____ x ____

L.C.M.: ____ x ____ x ____

= ________

Find the L.C.M. of each pair of numbers.

㉝ 10 15

L.C.M. : ________

㉞ 8 20

L.C.M. : ________

㉟ 9 24

L.C.M. : ________

㊱ 18 27

L.C.M. : ________

㊲ 22 33

L.C.M. : ________

㊳ 27 72

L.C.M. : ________

ACTIVITY

Read what Roger says. Then try out Goldbach's theory on the following numbers.

① 24 = _____ + _____

② 76 = _____ + _____

③ 90 = _____ + _____

A mathematician called Goldbach believes that all even numbers can be made by adding 2 prime numbers.
e.g. 10 = 7 + 3; 8 = 5 + 3

6 Time, Speed, and Distance

WORDS TO LEARN

a.m. – any time between midnight and midday (noon)
p.m. – any time between midday and midnight
24-hour clock time – telling times by using numerals only
e.g. 06:30 means 6:30 a.m.; 17:45 means 5:45 p.m.
Speed – how fast an object moves

$$\text{Speed} = \frac{\text{Distance}}{\text{Time}}$$

I travel 2400 km in 2 h. My speed is 1200 km/h.

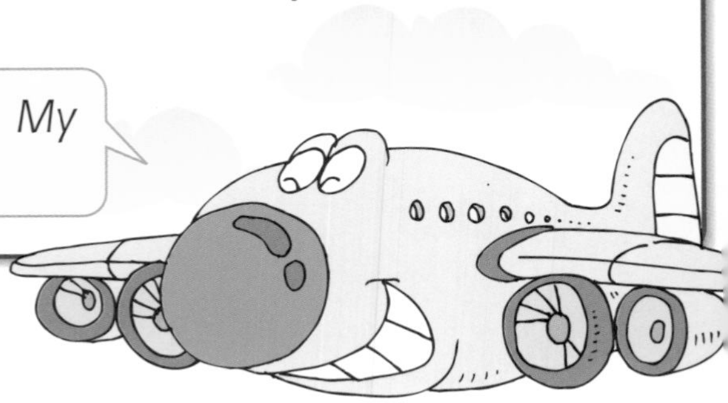

Write the times in 24-hour clock times.

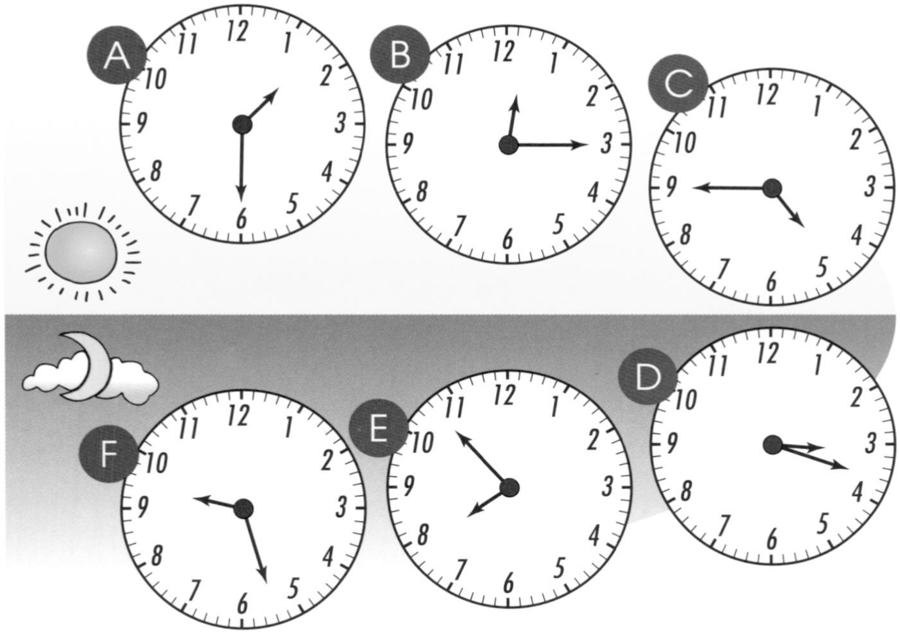

① A ____________
B ____________
C ____________
D ____________
E ____________
F ____________

Write the times using a.m. or p.m. and draw the clock hands to show the times.

②

③

Pearson International Airport

Flight	From	Scheduled Time	Arrival Time
CC34	Chicago	09:35	10:00
CP826	Munich	11:50	
CA68	New York		17:15
CA55	Vancouver	23:35	00:15

Look at the timetable. Solve the problems.

④ Did Flight CC34 arrive at the airport at night?

____

⑤ By how many minutes was Flight CA55 delayed?

____

⑥ What was the arrival time of Flight CP826 if there was a delay of 25 minutes? ____________

⑦ The arrival time of Flight CA68 was 36 minutes earlier than the scheduled time. What was the scheduled time? ____________

Peter and his father are at the airport. Help them solve the problems.

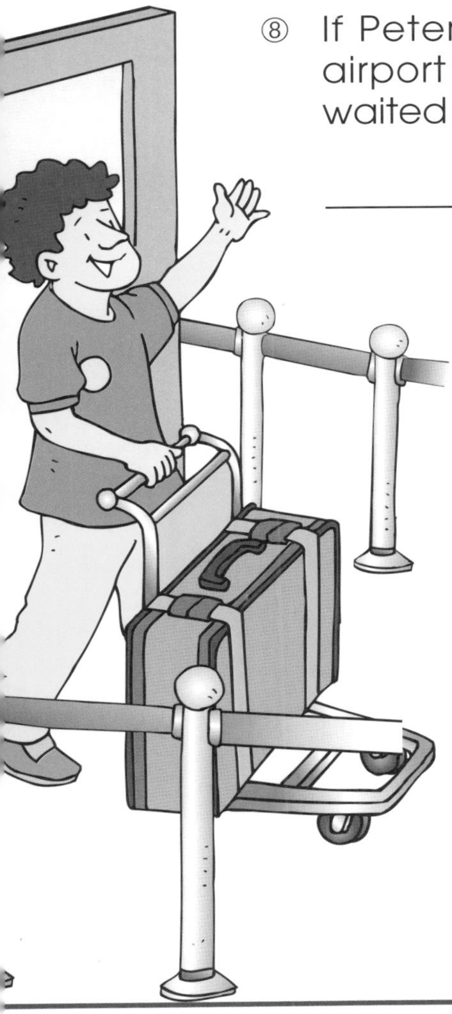

⑧ If Peter and his father arrived at the airport at 11:45, how long have they waited for Uncle Tim?

____

⑨ On which flight did Uncle Tim probably arrive?

____

⑩ How long did Uncle Tim take to go through customs?

____

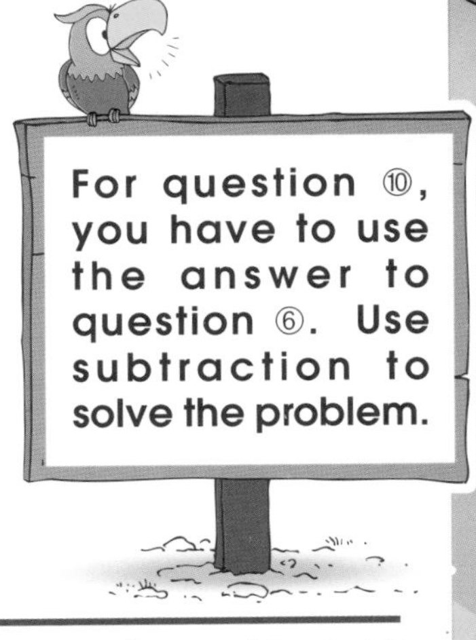

For question ⑩, you have to use the answer to question ⑥. Use subtraction to solve the problem.

6

Choose the most appropriate units to record the distances between the things or the lengths of the things. Write 'km', 'm', 'dm', 'cm' or 'mm'.

⑪

Fill in the blanks.

⑫ 63 cm = ______ mm

⑬ 4 km = ______ m

⑭ 9.2 m = ______ dm

⑮ 5.7 dm = ______ cm

⑯ 97 dm = ______ m

⑰ 2300 m = ______ km

⑱ 55 mm = ______ cm

⑲ 371 cm = ______ m

⑳ 105 m = ______ km

㉑ 0.8 m = ______ cm

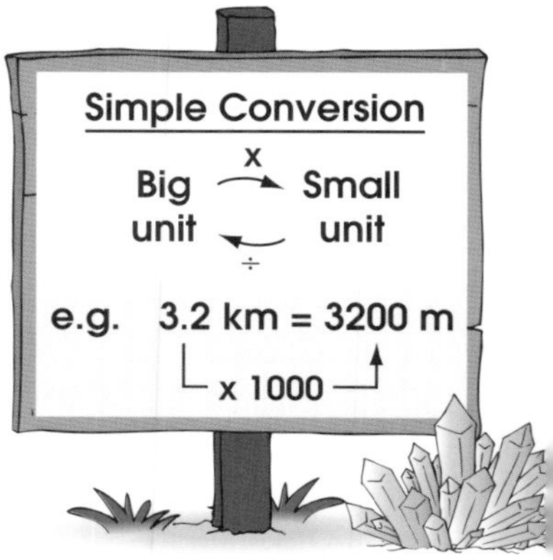

Simple Conversion
x
Big unit
Small unit
÷
e.g. 3.2 km = 3200 m
x 1000

Look at the picture. Solve the problems.

㉒ The distance between Alice's house and the baseball field is __________ m.

㉓ The distance from the baseball field to Tommy's house is half the distance between the baseball field and Alice's house. The distance from the baseball field to Tommy's house is __________ m.

㉔ Alice leaves her house and goes to Tommy's house passing through the baseball field. She has to travel __________ m in all.

Look at Andrew's record. Help him complete the table. Then answer the questions.

㉕

Race	Distance	Time	Speed
1	700 km	2 h	= (km/h)
2	347 000 m	1 h	= (km/h)
3		1.2 h	345 km/h
4		1.5 h	354 km/h

$$\text{Speed} = \frac{\text{Distance}}{\text{Time}}$$

e.g. Travelling 150 km in 2 h.
Speed:
150 ÷ 2 = 75 (km/h)

㉖ In which race did Andrew drive at the highest speed? ____________

㉗ How many more kilometres will be covered in 1 hour if Andrew drives at the speed in Race 1 instead of the speed in Race 3? ____________

㉘ If Andrew takes only 1 hour to complete Race 3, what will his speed be? ____________

㉙ If Ted walks at a speed of 4 m/s to the race course, a distance of 2160 m, how long will it take him to reach there?

____

㉚ If Ted starts walking to the race course at 11:58 a.m., at what time will he reach the race course?

____

For question ㉙, use division to find the answer.

$$\text{Time} = \frac{\text{Distance}}{\text{Speed}}$$

ACTIVITY

Look at the picture. What is the distance between the turtle and the snail after 2 minutes?

____

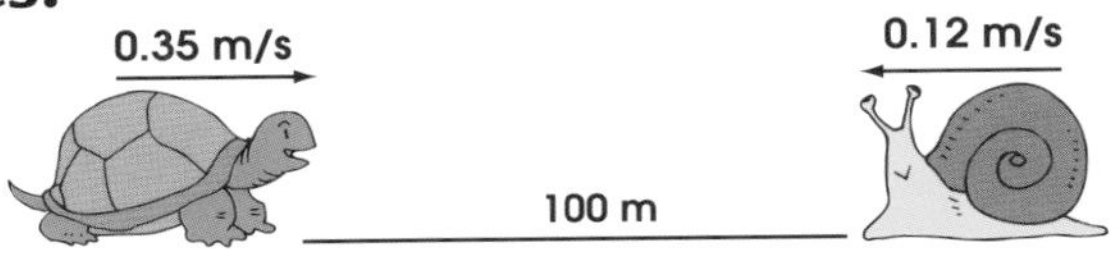

7 Perimeter and Area

WORDS TO LEARN

Perimeter – the distance around the outside of a shape
Area – the number of square units of a surface

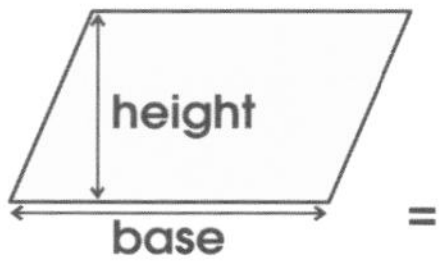

Area of a parallelogram
= base x height

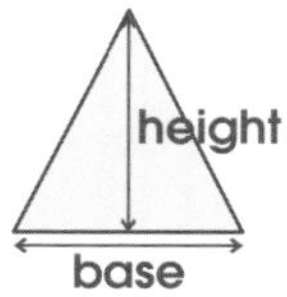

Area of a triangle
= base x height ÷ 2

Look at the shapes. Complete the table and answer the questions.

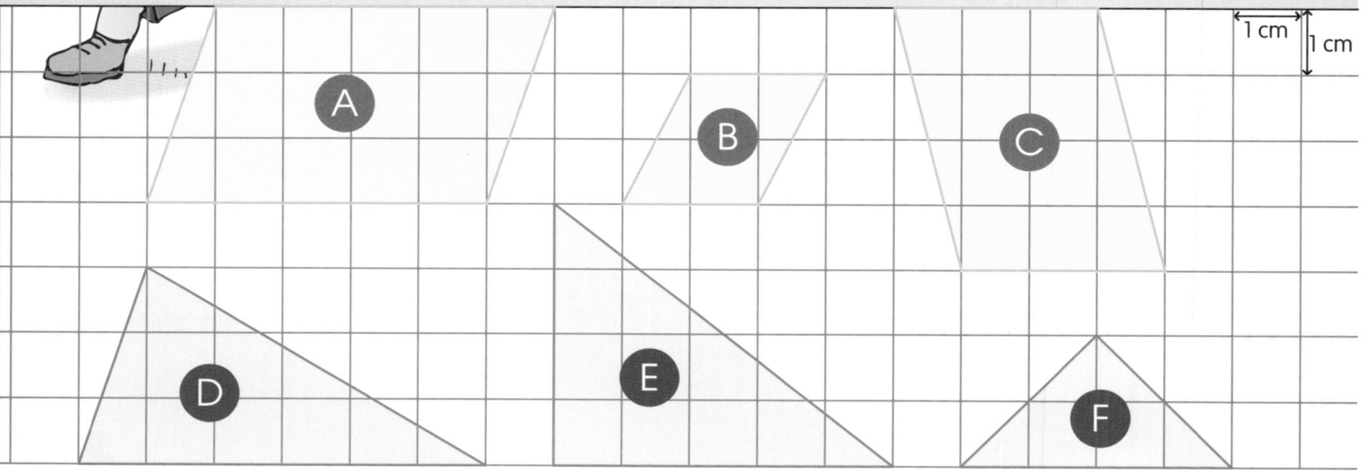

①

	Base	Height	Area
A			
B			
C			
D			
E			
F			

② Is the product of the base and height of a parallelogram the same as its area?

____

③ Is half of the product of the base and height of a triangle the same as its area?

____

See how Jimmy cuts a parallelogram. Then find the base, height, area, and perimeter of each of the parallelograms.

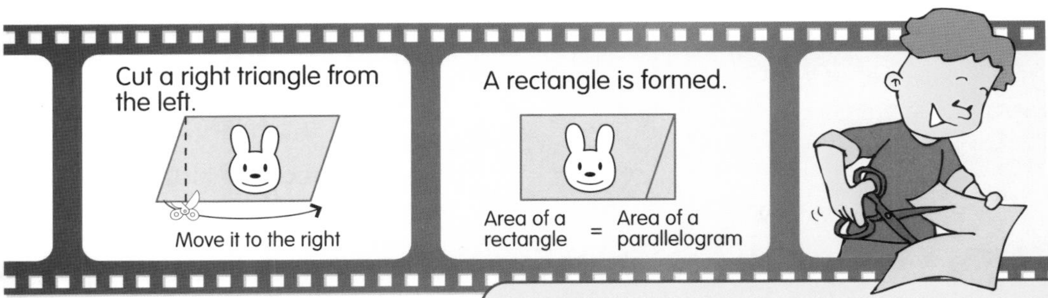

Cut a right triangle from the left.
Move it to the right
A rectangle is formed.
Area of a rectangle = Area of a parallelogram

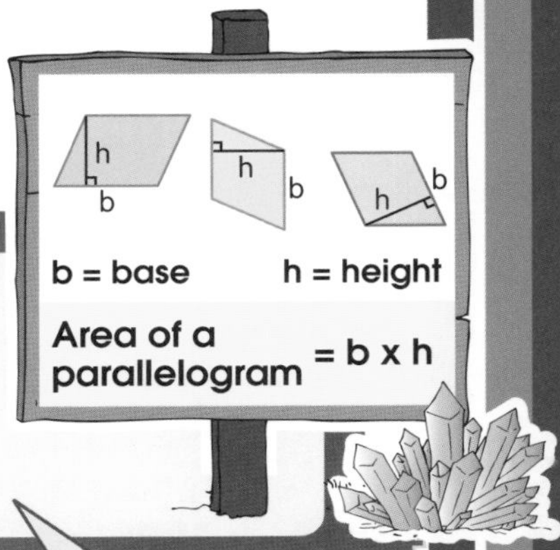

Find the perimeter of a parallelogram by adding the 4 sides.

④

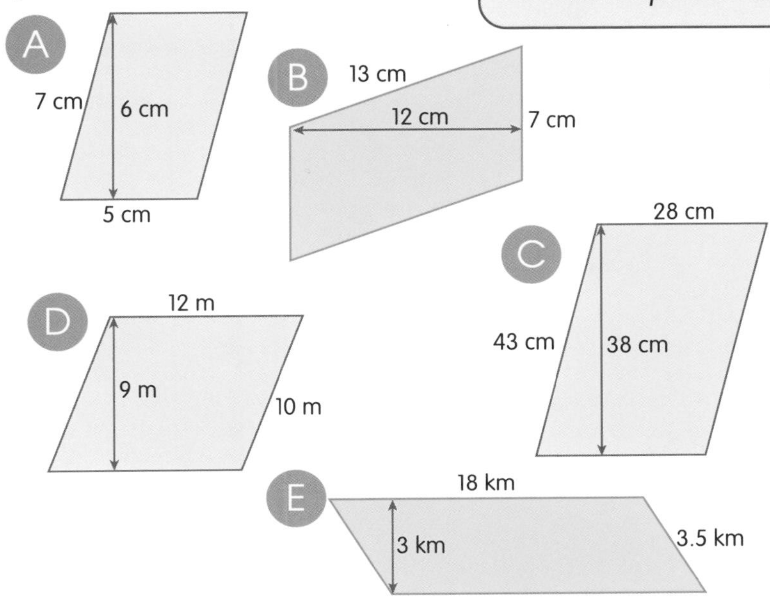

	Base	Height	Area	Perimeter
A				
B				
C				
D				
E				

Draw the parallelograms on the grid as specified. Then colour them.

⑤ The green parallelogram has a base of 6 cm and a height of 5 cm. The area of the red parallelogram is 9 cm^2.

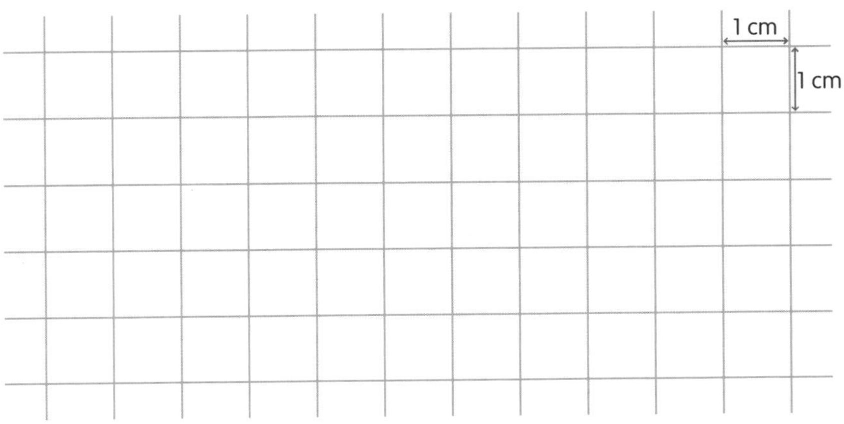

Read what Karen says. Then find the base, height, area, and perimeter of each of the triangles.

⑥

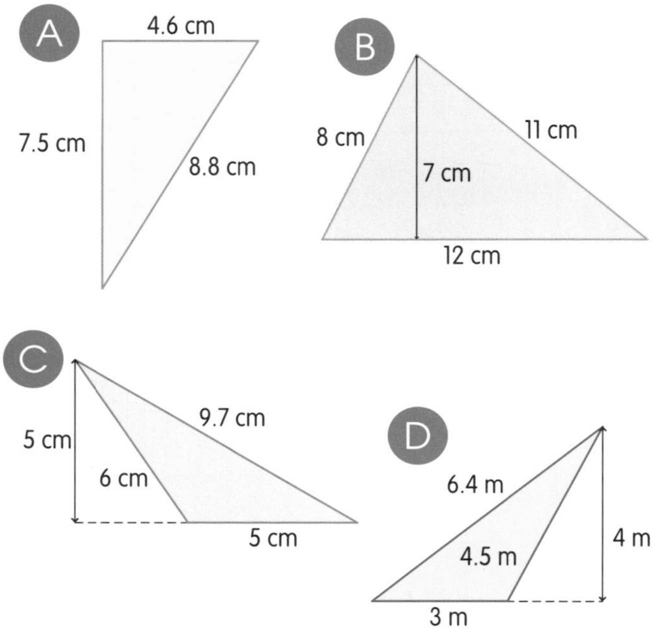

	Base	Height	Area	Perimeter
A				
B				
C				
D				

Look at the triangles in each group. Put the letters in order. Start with the one that has the greatest area.

If the bases of the triangles are the same, the one with the tallest height is the greatest.

⑦

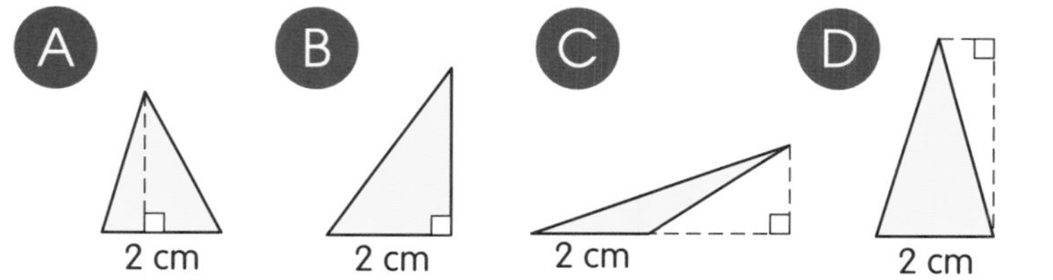

The order: ______________________

⑧

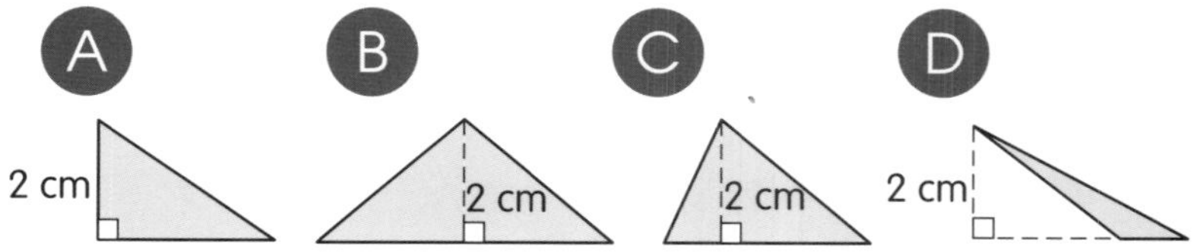

The order: ______________________

Draw 3 different triangles with each having an area of 12 cm².

⑨

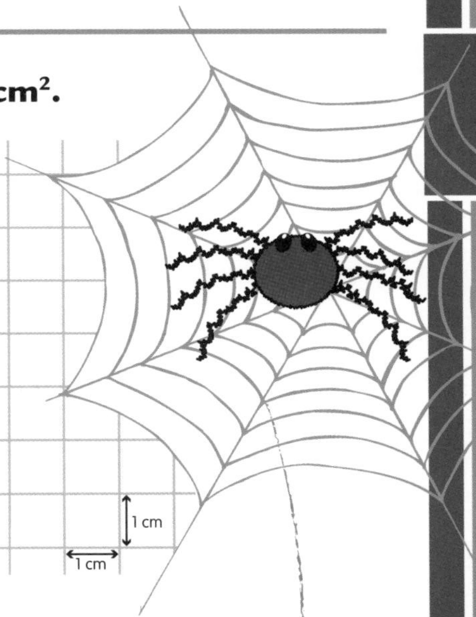

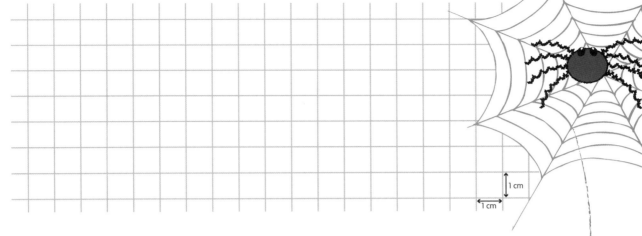

Look at the shapes. Solve the problems.

⑩ If the area of the parallelogram is 39 cm^2, what is its base?

_______ cm

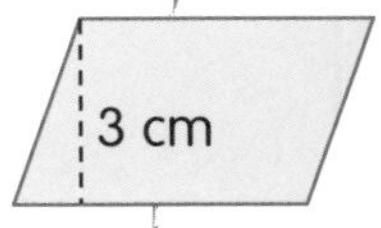

⑪ If the base of the triangle is 2 times its height, what is its area?

_______ cm^2

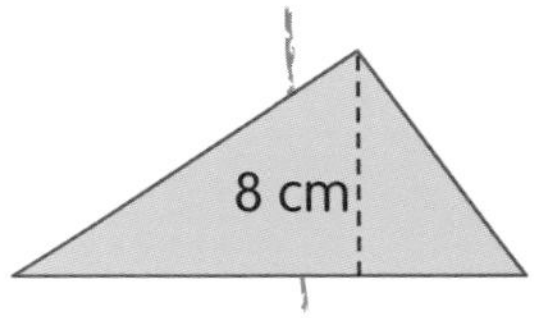

⑫ If Speedy the Spider wants to get the greatest triangle from the cardboard, what is the area of that triangle?

_______ cm^2

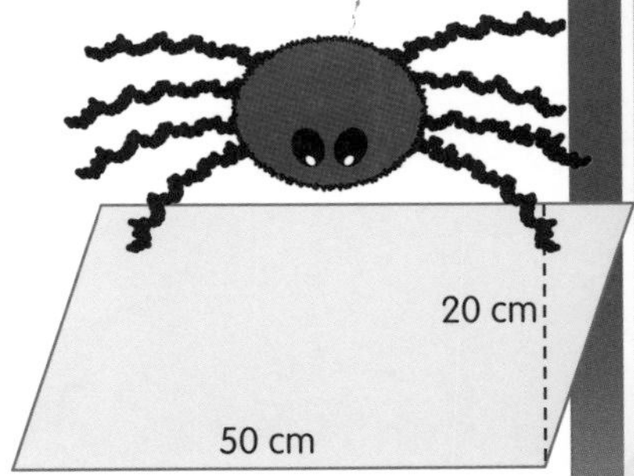

Find the area of the coloured part.

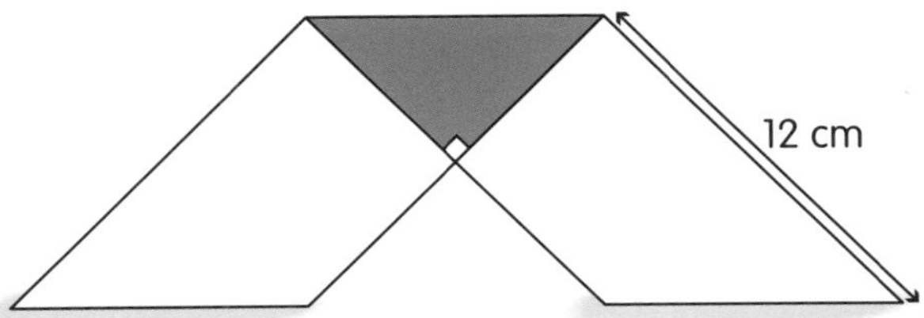

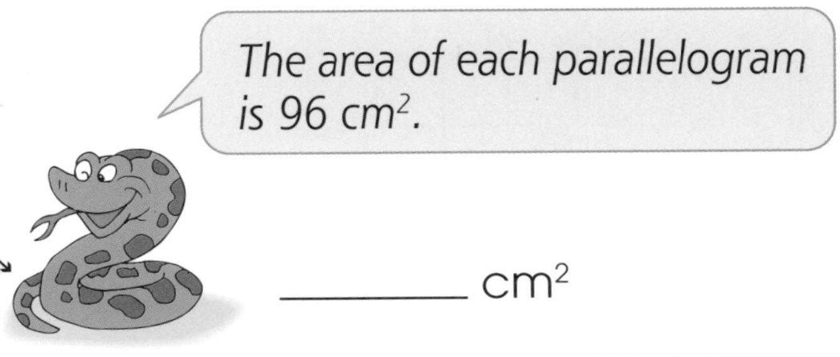

The area of each parallelogram is 96 cm².

_______ cm^2

8 2-D Shapes and 3-D Figures

WORDS TO LEARN

Line of symmetry – a line that cuts a shape into halves

Rotational symmetry – a figure has rotational symmetry if it fits on itself within a complete rotation

Order of rotational symmetry – the number of times the figure fits on itself in one complete rotation

This windmill has rotational symmetry of order 4.

Net – a 2-D shape which can be folded into a 3-D figure

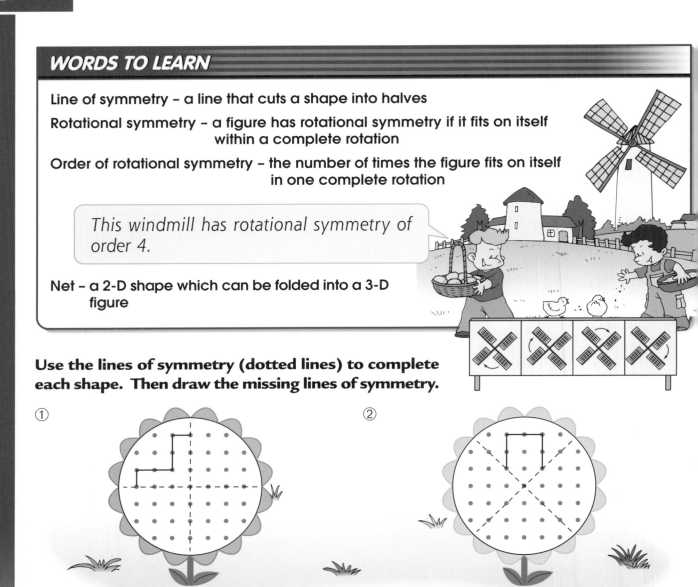

Use the lines of symmetry (dotted lines) to complete each shape. Then draw the missing lines of symmetry.

①

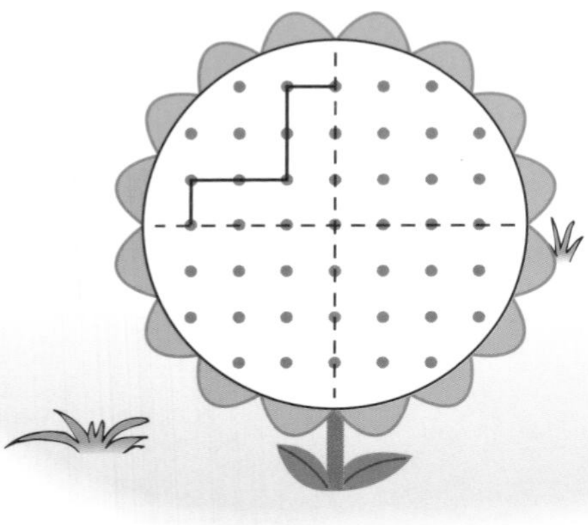

②

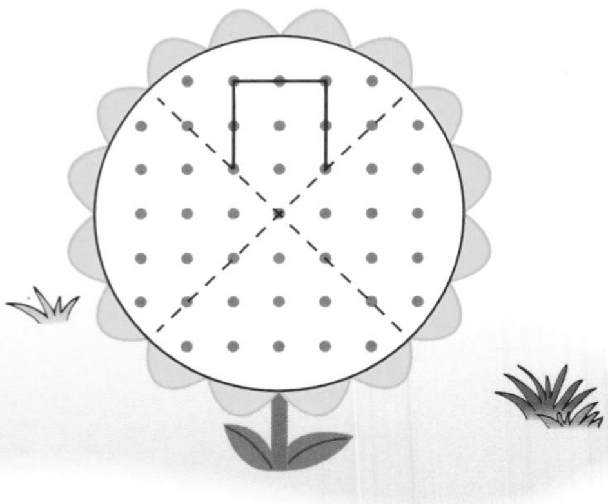

Add three squares to each shape to make it symmetrical. Then draw the line(s) of symmetry.

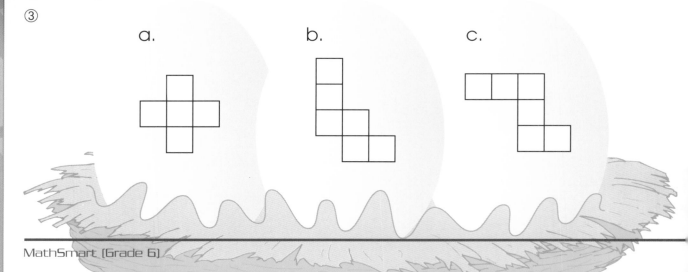

③

a.

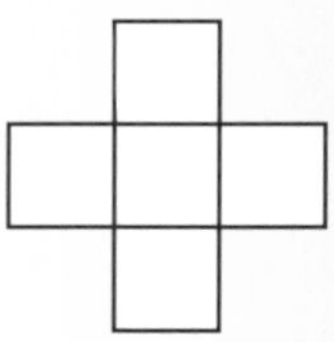

b.

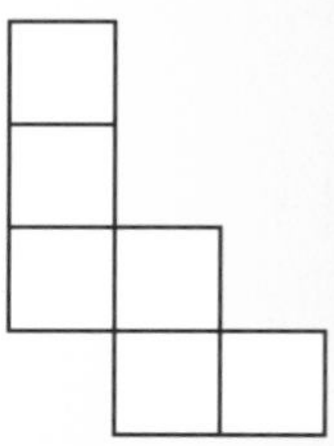

c.

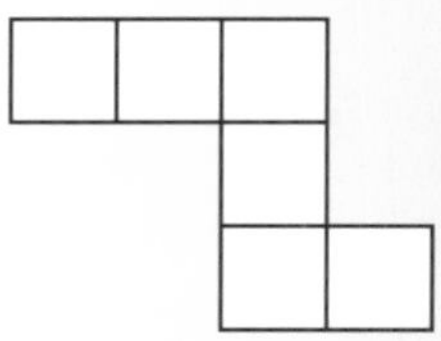

Help the clown write the order of rotational symmetry for each shape on the line.

④

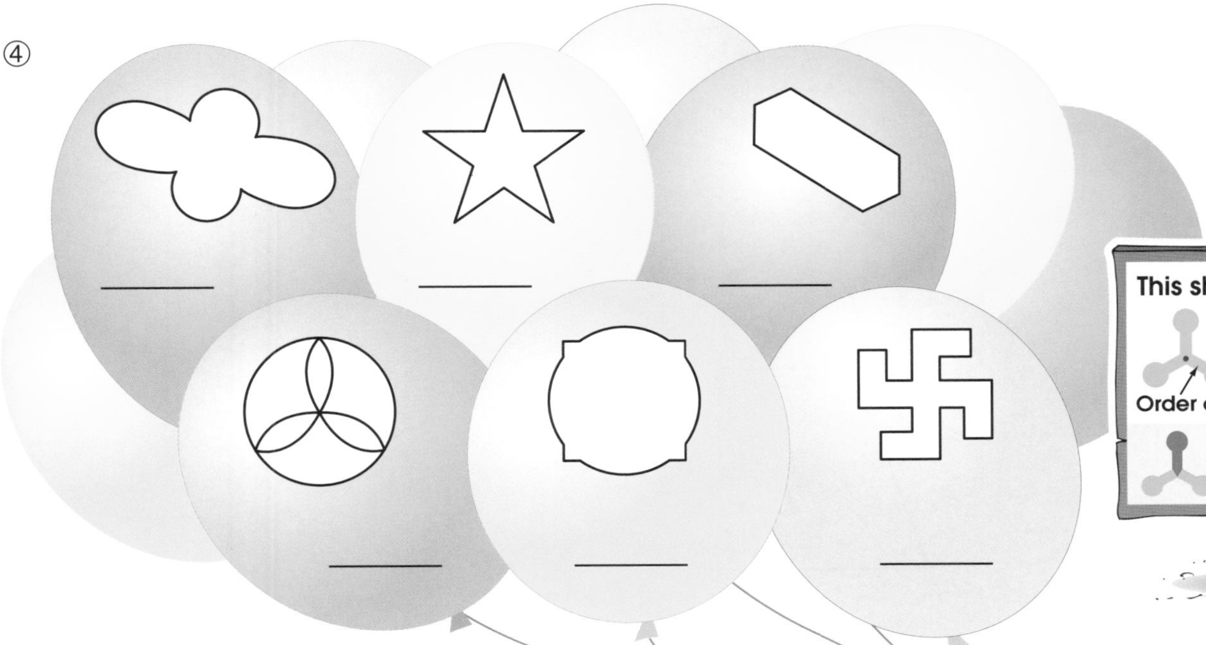

This shape fits on itself 3 times within a complete rotation.
Order of 3

Use a protractor and a ruler to construct the shapes. Then label them with letters.

⑤

- **A** A triangle with no rotational symmetry
- **B** A triangle with angles 45°, 45°, and 90°
- **C** A rectangle with sides 6 cm and 3 cm, and can be cut into 8 identical squares
- **D** A parallelogram with base 6 cm and height 5 cm, and can be cut into 5 identical parallelograms

Draw a congruent figure for each shape.

⑥

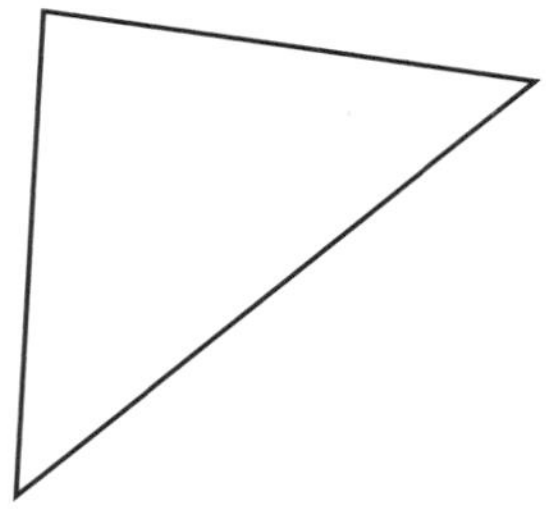

⑦

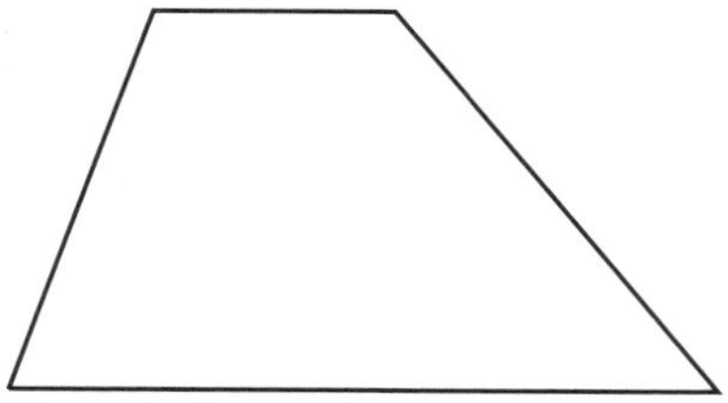

Fill in the blanks with numbers to complete what Joseph says. Then help him draw the missing parts of each net.

⑧

A rectangular pyramid 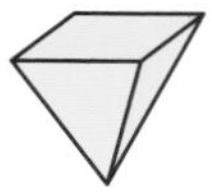 has ______ rectangular face(s) and ______ triangular face(s).

A hexagonal prism 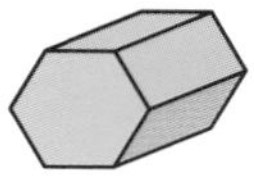 has ______ hexagonal face(s) and ______ rectangular face(s).

⑨

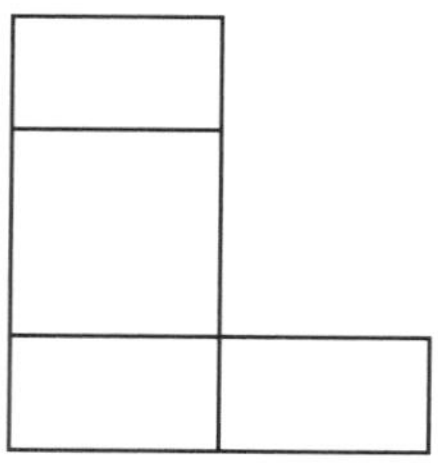

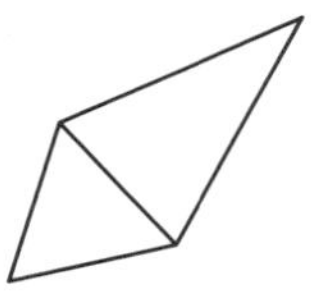

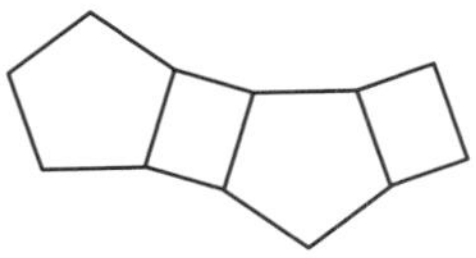

Rectangular Prism

Triangular Pyramid

Pentagonal Prism

Check ✔ the correct letters.

⑩ Which quadrilaterals have 2 pairs of parallel sides?

(A) Square (B) Trapezoid (C) Rhombus

⑪ Which triangle has 2 equal sides only?

(A) Equilateral (B) Scalene (C) Isosceles

⑫ Which shapes have no right angles?

(A) Rhombus (B) Rectangle (C) Parallelogram

Draw the models on the isometric dot paper.

⑬

ACTIVITY

Are the triangles similar? Measure the angles of each triangle. Then explain.

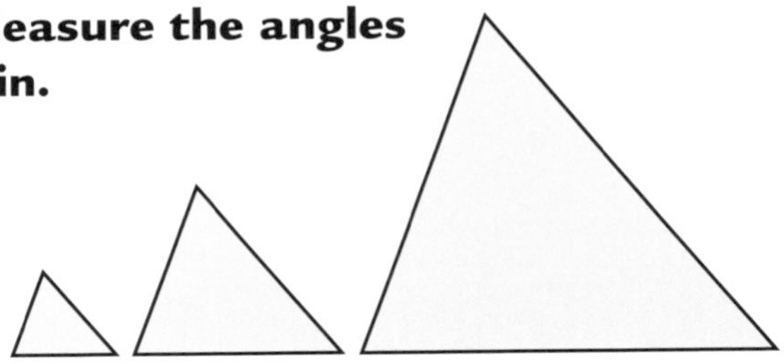

____

____

Midway Test

Use the property of multiplication to do the questions. (2 marks)

① 9 x (8 + 7)

= 9 x ____ + 9 x ____

= ____ + ____

= ____

② (116 – 29) x 3

= 116 x ____ – 29 x ____

= ____ – ____

= ____

Solve the problems. (8 marks)

③ 34 ÷ (19 – 2)

=

④ 18 + 8 x 10

=

⑤ 22 x 5 – 60

=

⑥ (43 + 7) ÷ 2

=

Write the first eight multiples of each pair of numbers. Then find their common multiple (s) and L.C.M. (8 marks)

⑦ 7 : ____ , ____ , ____ , ____ , ____ , ____ , ____ , ____

8 : ____ , ____ , ____ , ____ , ____ , ____ , ____ , ____

Common multiple(s) : ____________ L.C.M. : ________

⑧ 6 : ____ , ____ , ____ , ____ , ____ , ____ , ____ , ____

9 : ____ , ____ , ____ , ____ , ____ , ____ , ____ , ____

Common multiple(s) : ____________ L.C.M. : ________

Find the answers. (14 marks)

⑨ $25\overline{)9150}$

⑩ $37\overline{)2833}$

⑪
$$\begin{array}{r} 782 \\ \times \quad 32 \\ \hline \end{array}$$

⑫ 695 x 47 = ________

⑬ 8001 ÷ 19 = ________

⑭ 29 x 163 = ________

⑮ 5107 ÷ 23 = ________

Look at the map. Then fill in the blanks. (6 marks)

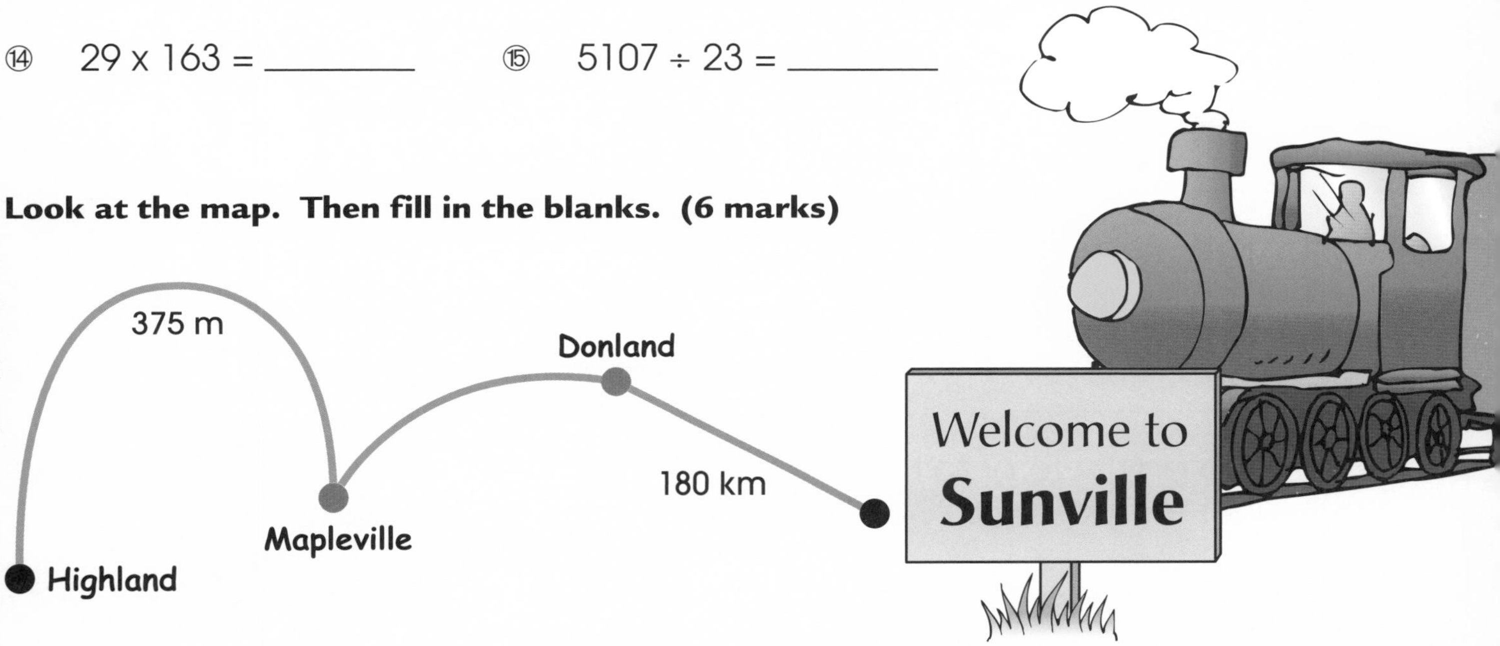

⑯ The train takes 2 h to travel from Sunville to Donland. What is the travelling speed?

____

⑰ If the train keeps the above speed and takes 2.5 h to travel from Donland to Mapleville, what is the distance between these two cities?

____

⑱ The train leaves Mapleville at a speed of 75 km/h at 13:05. At what time will it arrive at Highland?

____

Midway Test

Find the factors of the numbers in each group. Then find their common factor(s) and G.C.F. (8 marks)

⑲

20 : ____________________

32 : ____________________

Common factors : ________

G.C.F. : ______

⑳

18 : ____________________

24 : ____________________

Common factors : ________

G.C.F. : ______

Look at the weather forecast. Answer the questions. (3 marks)

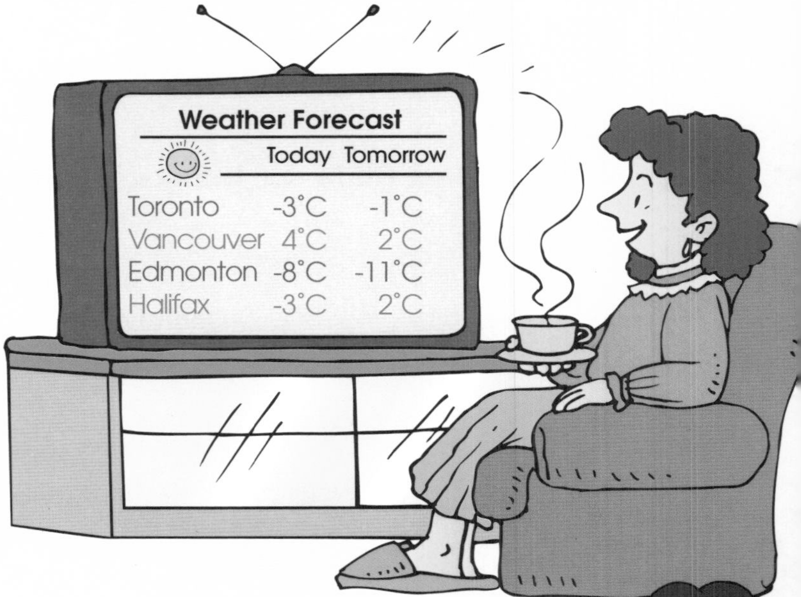

Weather Forecast
Today Tomorrow
Toronto -3°C -1°C
Vancouver 4°C 2°C
Edmonton -8°C -11°C
Halifax -3°C 2°C

㉑ What is the temperature of Halifax today?

____

㉒ Is the temperature of Edmonton higher than that of Toronto today?

____

㉓ Which day in Toronto has a higher temperature?

____

Help George draw the shapes. (4 marks)

㉔ A triangle with 3 lines of symmetry

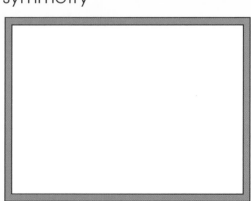

㉕ A parallelogram with base 5 cm and height 3 cm

Write each number as a product of prime factors. Then find the L.C.M. and G.C.F. of each pair of numbers. (㉖ 6 marks, ㉗ – ㉚ 8 marks)

㉖ a. b. c.

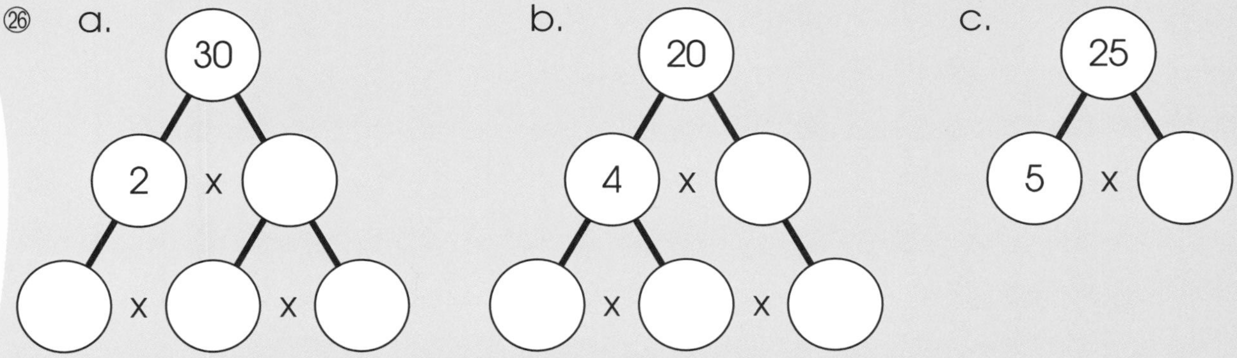

30 = ____________ 20 = ____________ 25 = ____________

㉗ The G.C.F. of 20 and 30 is ________ .

㉘ The G.C.F. of 25 and 30 is ________ .

㉙ The L.C.M. of 20 and 30 is ________ .

㉚ The L.C.M. of 20 and 25 is ________ .

Write the order of rotational symmetry for each shape. (2 marks)

㉛

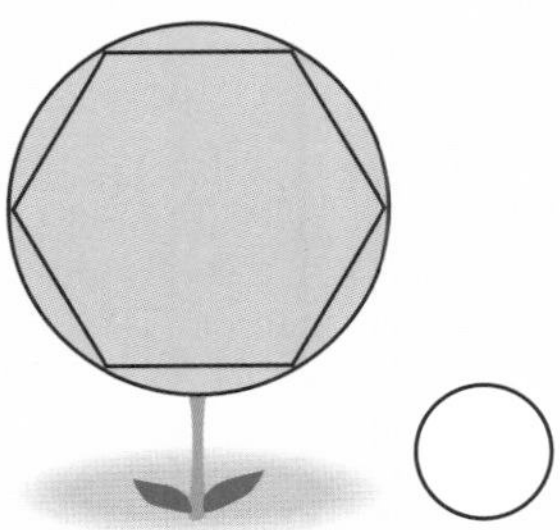

㉜

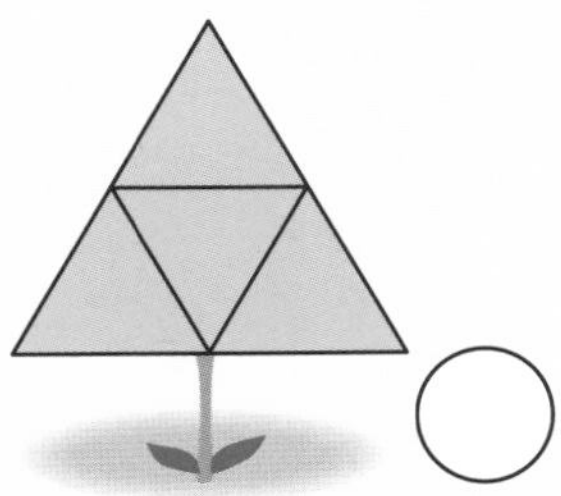

Find the answers. (4 marks)

㉝ 42 066 – 6997 = ________

㉞ 395 + 285 + 98 + 122 = ________

㉟ 90 303 – 2455 = ________

㊱ 898 + 302 + 788 + 477 = ________

Midway Test

Find the area and the perimeter of each shape. (8 marks)

(37)

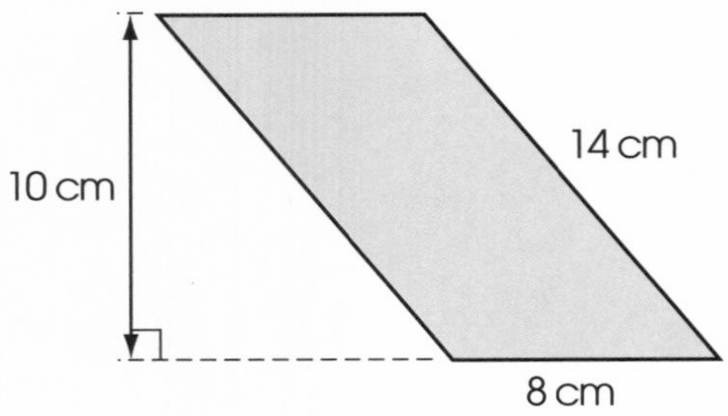

Area = ____________

Perimeter = ____________

(38)

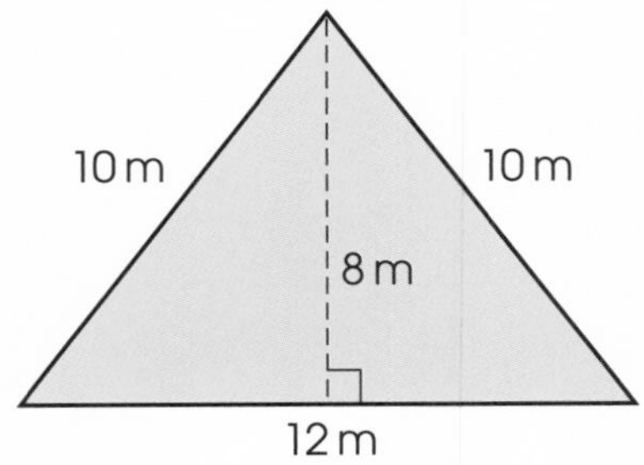

Area = ____________

Perimeter = ____________

Draw a parallelogram and a triangle each having an area of 16 cm². (2 marks)

(39)

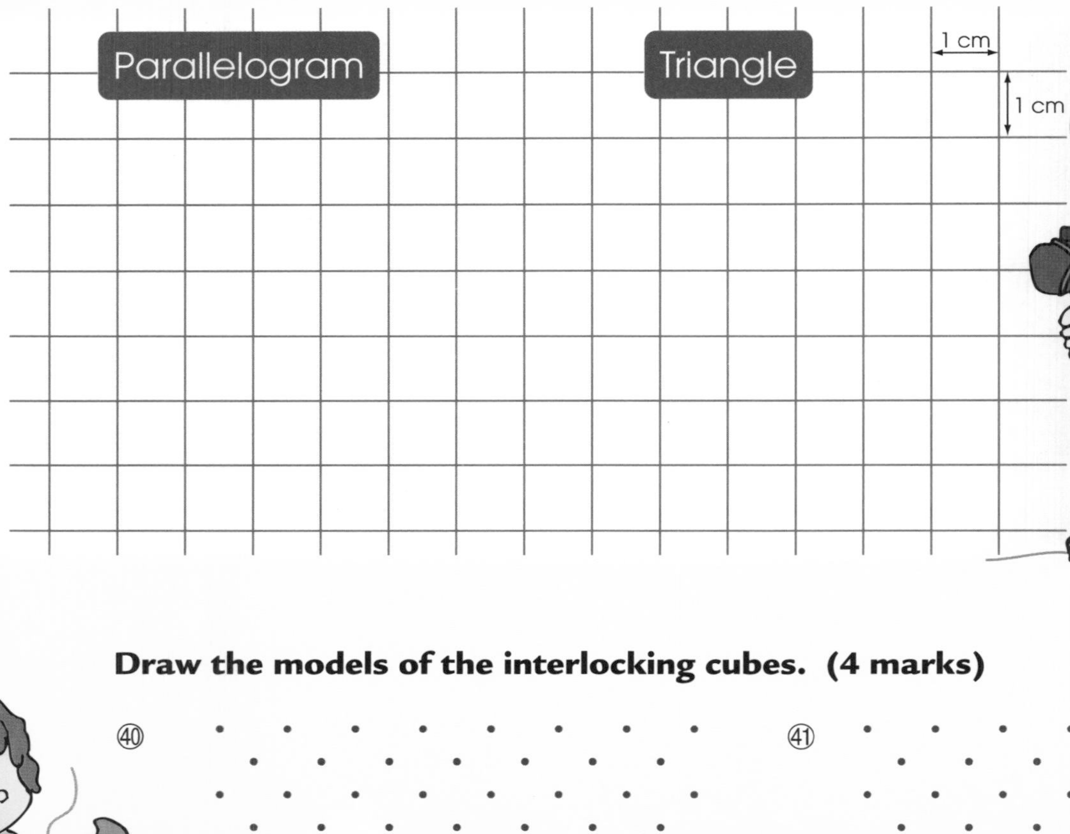

Draw the models of the interlocking cubes. (4 marks)

(40)

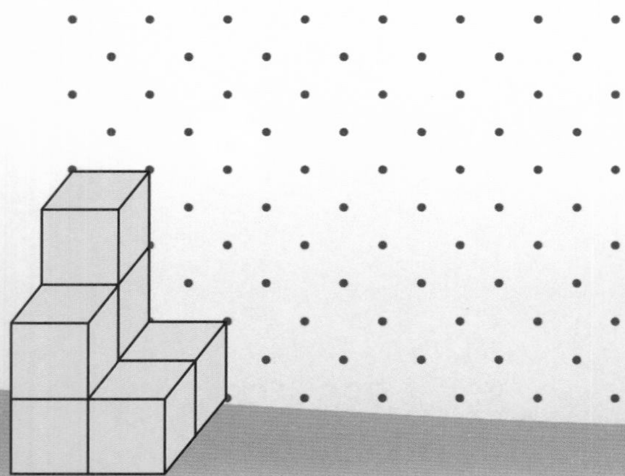

(41)

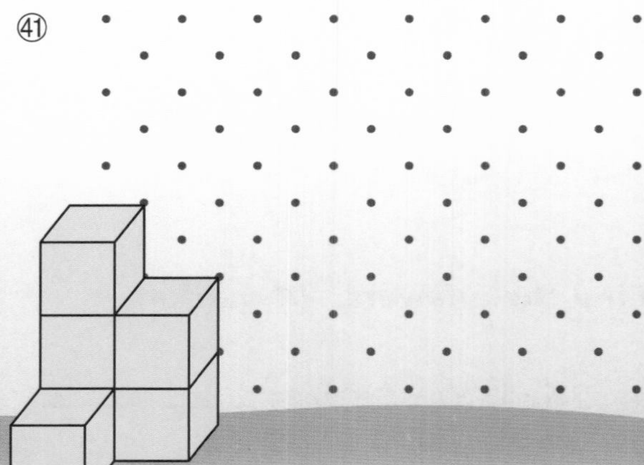

Use the lines of symmetry (red lines) to complete each shape. Then draw one congruent figure for each symmetrical shape. (4 marks)

42 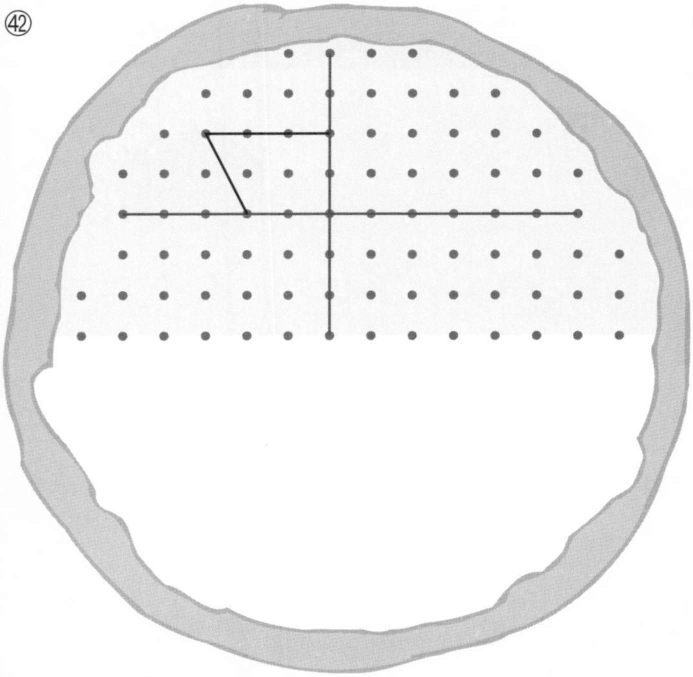

43 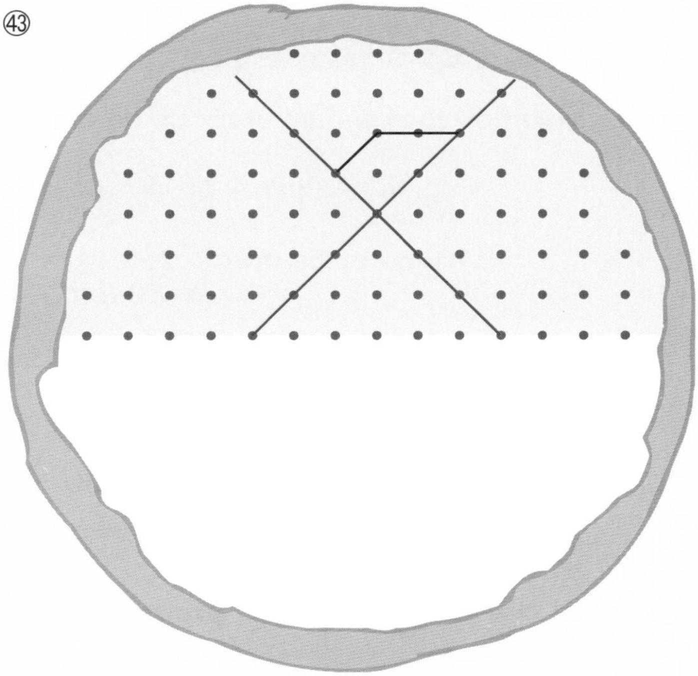

Solve the problems. (9 marks)

44. How much will Uncle Philip make from selling 927 pizzas?

45. Uncle Philip expects to earn $13 000 next month. If he is going to earn $4662 less than expected, how much will he earn next month?

46. If 3348 pizzas are sold in March, how many pizzas are sold in a day on average?

9 Volume and Mass

WORDS TO LEARN

Volume – the amount of space an object takes up

Volume of a prism: Base Area x Height

Volume of the prism: 25 x 14
= 350 (cm^3)

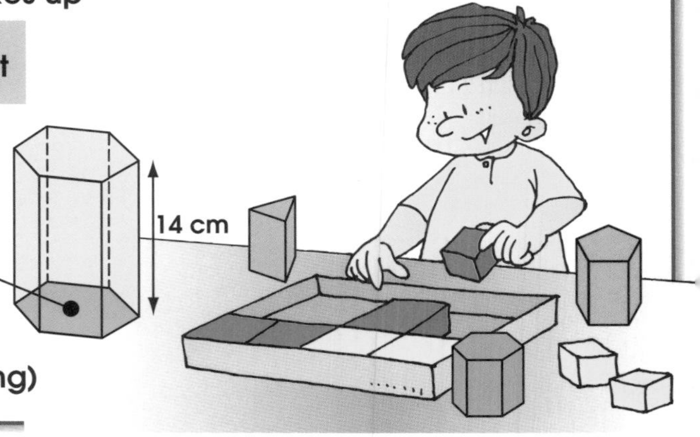

Mass – units for measuring mass:
Kilogram (kg), Gram (g), Milligram (mg)

Find the volume of each prism.

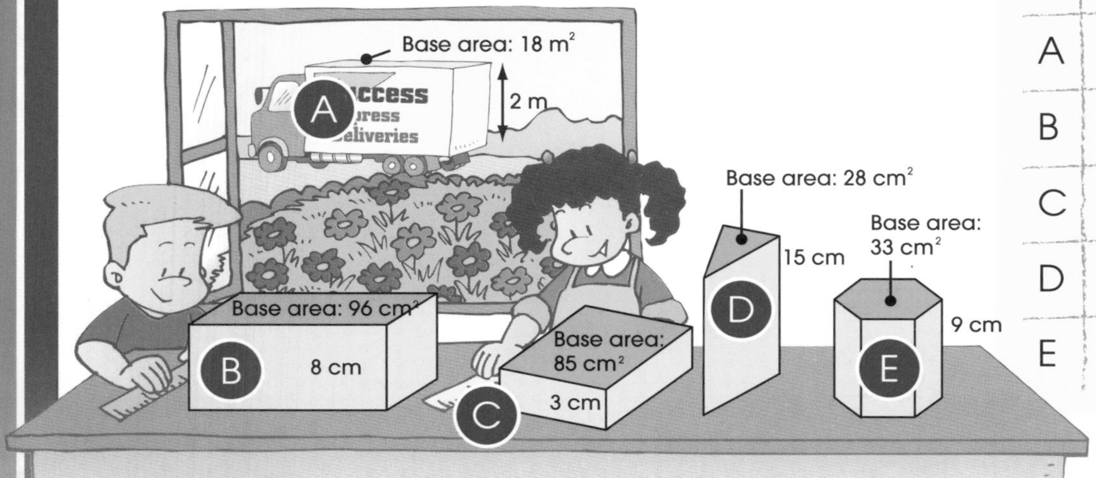

①	Volume
A	
B	
C	
D	
E	

Help Joey the Cat solve the problems.

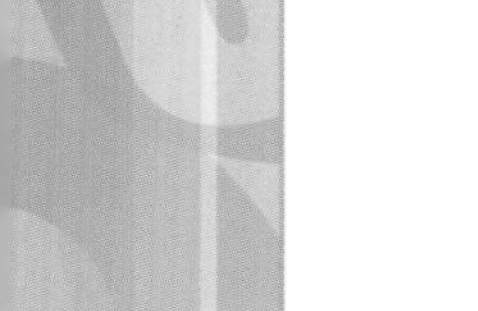

② A box measures 8 cm by 9 cm by 4.5 cm. What is its volume? ________ cm^3

③ What is the volume of each solid?

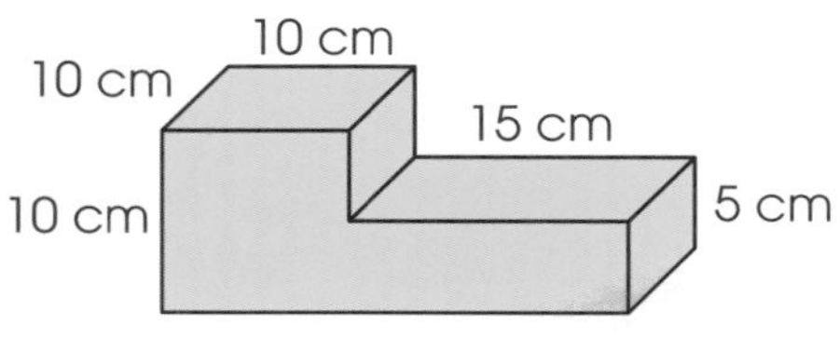

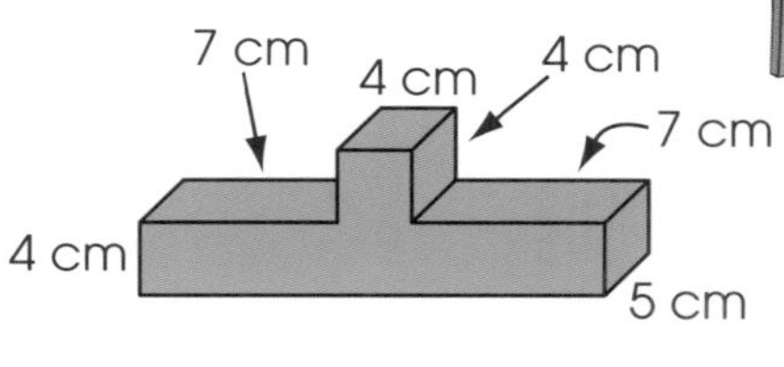

________ cm^3 ________ cm^3

Fill in the blanks.

④ 9 kg + 8 g = ________ g

⑤ 2510 g + 1880 g = ________ kg

⑥ 6 g + 145 mg = ________ mg

⑦ 33 mg + 945 mg = ________ g

⑧ 8 g + 9.24 g = ________ mg

⑨ 0.65 kg + 250 g = ________ kg

⑩ 1.2 kg + 60 g = ________ g

⑪ 1726 mg + 0.274 g = ________ g

Read what Timothy says. Find the weight of each alien and write the answers on their T-shirts. Then answer the questions.

George is 500 g less than 8 kg. The total weight of George and Louis is 15.5 kg. If Wayne gains 5 mg, he will weigh 1 g. Ted is 5 times as heavy as Wayne. Richard is 2.9 kg lighter than Louis. Bob is 0.225 g heavier than Ted.

⑫

⑬ Who is the heaviest? ________

⑭ Who is the lightest? ________

ACTIVITY

Read what Ray says. Help him solve the problem.

The total weight of 3 balls and myself is 886 g. If I weigh 400 mg, how much does each ball weigh?

________ g

10 Operations with Decimals

WORDS TO LEARN

Decimal – a numeral containing a decimal point with the value of digits to the right of the decimal point being less than 1

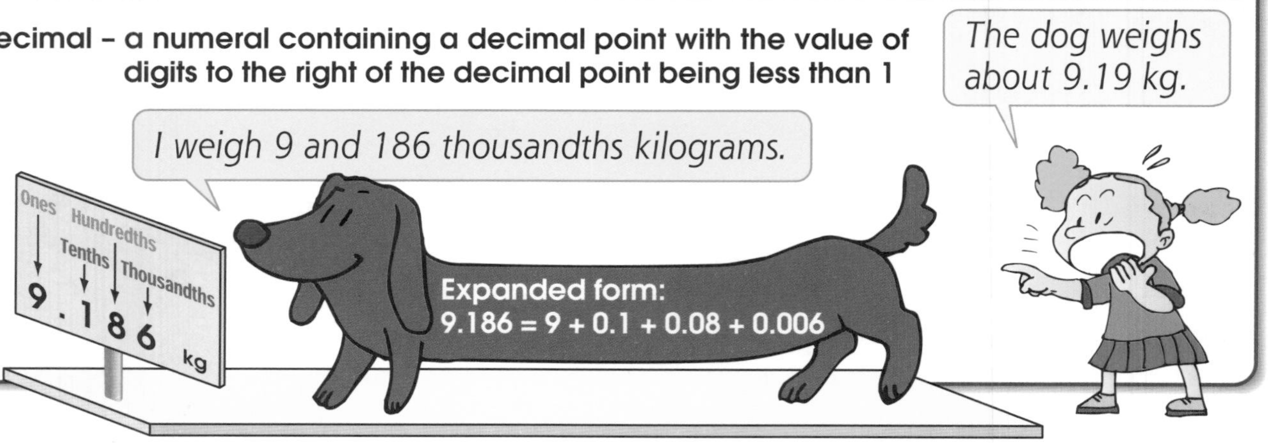

The dog weighs about 9.19 kg.
I weigh 9 and 186 thousandths kilograms.
Ones
Hundredths
Tenths
Thousandths
9 . 1 8 6
kg
Expanded form:
9.186 = 9 + 0.1 + 0.08 + 0.006

Write the decimals in expanded form and in words.

① 45.619 Expanded form: ____________________

In words: ____________________

② 60.202 Expanded form: ____________________

In words: ____________________

Find the answers.

③
$$\begin{array}{r} 6.8 \\ -\ 2.549 \\ \hline \end{array}$$

④
$$\begin{array}{r} 3.175 \\ +\ 0.856 \\ \hline \end{array}$$

⑤
$$\begin{array}{r} 4.017 \\ -\ 3.85 \\ \hline \end{array}$$

⑥ 9.14 + 2.889 = ________

⑦ 3.46 – 0.875 = ________

⑧ 4.06 – 3.451 = ________

⑨ 7.07 + 1.864 = ________

⑩ If Susan weighs 28.64 kg, her cat weighs ________ kg.

⑪ If Susan's cat gains 0.524 kg, it will weigh ________ kg.

Find the products or quotients mentally.

⑫ 2.623 x 100 = ________ ⑬ 3.88 ÷ 10 = ________

⑭ 89.4 ÷ 100 = ________ ⑮ 0.767 x 100 = ________

⑯ 5.051 x 10 = ________ ⑰ 305.4 ÷ 100 = ________

⑱ 6.25 ÷ 100 = ________ ⑲ 1 ÷ 1000 = ________

Multiply – move the (•) to the right
Divide – move the (•) to the left
2.93 x 100 = 293
Move it 2 places to the right.
$0.95 1 kg
$1.28 1 kg
Decimals x Decimals
The no. of decimal places in the product is equal to the total no. of decimal places in the two numerals.
e.g. 3.6
x 0.8
2.88

Help Mrs. Martin solve the problems.

⑳ How much do 2.6 kg of apples cost?

$$\begin{array}{rrl} & 0.95 & \leftarrow \text{2 decimal places} \\ \times & 2.6 & \leftarrow \text{1 decimal place} \\ \hline & 570 & \\ & 1900 & \\ \hline & \square.\square\square\square & \leftarrow \text{3 decimal places} \end{array}$$

2.6 kg of apples cost $ ________ .

㉑
$$\begin{array}{rr} & 4.2 \\ \times & 0.6 \\ \hline \end{array}$$

㉒
$$\begin{array}{rr} & 3.25 \\ \times & 0.8 \\ \hline \end{array}$$

㉓
$$\begin{array}{rr} & 4.668 \\ \times & 3 \\ \hline \end{array}$$

㉔ 6.27 x 1.8 = ________ ㉕ 3.5 x 2.66 = ________

㉖ 4.15 x 6.3 = ________ ㉗ 10.2 x 3.17 = ________

㉘ 8.06 x 1.4 = ________ ㉙ 2.19 x 8.5 = ________

㉚ 3.8 kg of apples cost $ ________ (Correct to 1 decimal place.).

㉛ 4.7 kg of mangoes cost $ ________ (Correct to 2 decimal places.).

㉜ 1.5 kg of mangoes cost $ ________ (Correct to 2 decimal places.).

Follow Elaine's method to do the division.

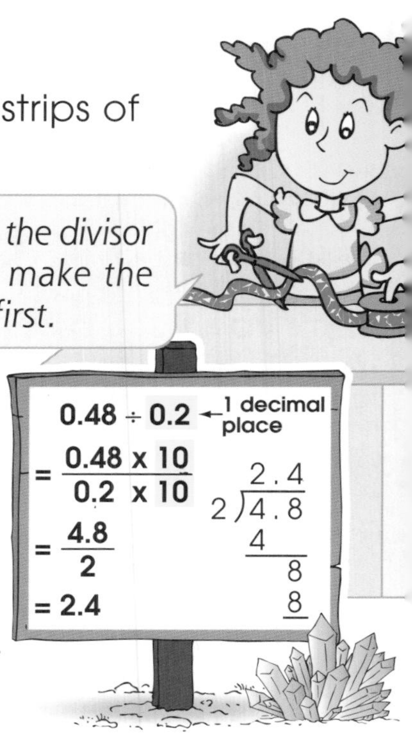
0.48 ÷ 0.2 ← 1 decimal place
= 0.48 x 10 / 0.2 x 10
= 4.8 / 2
= 2.4
2.4
2) 4.8
4
8
8

Multiply the dividend and the divisor by 10, 100, or 1000 to make the divisor a whole number first.

33 Elaine wants to cut a 0.75-m long ribbon into strips of 0.15 m each. How many strips can she get?

$0.75 \div 0.15 = \frac{0.75}{0.15}$

$= \frac{0.75 \times 100}{0.15 \times 100}$

$= \frac{\quad}{15}$

= ______

15) 75

______

She can get ______ strips.

34 $32.4 \div 0.4$

$= \frac{32.4 \times \quad}{0.4 \times \quad}$

$= \frac{\quad}{4}$

= ______

4) ______

35 $1.6 \div 0.08$

$= \frac{1.6 \times \quad}{0.08 \times \quad}$

$= \frac{\quad}{8}$

= ______

8) ______

36 $8.85 \div 0.05 =$ ______

37 $3.45 \div 0.23 =$ ______

38 $0.221 \div 1.3 =$ ______

39 $29.45 \div 1.9 =$ ______

40 $16.74 \div 2.7 =$ ______

41 $12.18 \div 0.87 =$ ______

42 Each roll of ribbon costs $0.95. How many rolls of ribbon can Tony buy with $17.10?

______ rolls of ribbon

43 1.5 m of ribbon is needed to tie a gift box. How many gift boxes can be tied with 13.5 m of ribbon?

______ gift boxes

Find the answers.

When an expression involves '+' and '–' or '×' and '÷', solve the problem from left to right.
e.g. 3.3 × 4 ÷ 0.2 = 13.2 ÷ 0.2
= 66

44. 3.2 + 1.4 – 0.58 = ______

45. 6.4 ÷ 0.4 × 1.3 = ______

46. 3.84 – 1.765 + 2.339 = ______

47. 6.447 + 1.385 – 2.608 = ______

48. 3.5 × 1.9 ÷ 0.5 = ______

49. 8.91 ÷ 2.7 × 1.44 = ______

50. 17.8 × 4.2 ÷ 2.8 = ______

Solve the problems.

51. A boat covered a distance of 32.8 km in 1 h. It covers ________ km in 2.4 h.

52. Peter travelled 3.258 km on Monday and 4.165 km on Tuesday. He travelled ________ km in the past two days.

53. Sister Shark weighs 68.259 kg. If Sister Shark is 6.84 kg lighter than Brother Shark, Brother Shark weighs ________ kg.

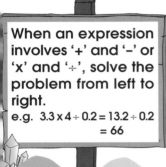

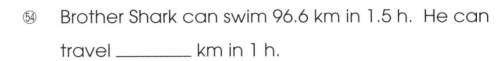

54. Brother Shark can swim 96.6 km in 1.5 h. He can travel ________ km in 1 h.

55. Sister Shark is 0.87 m long. If Brother Shark is 1.2 times as long as Sister Shark, he is ________ m long.

ACTIVITY

Work out the answers mentally.

1. 23.5 ÷ 23.5 + 1 = ______

2. 12.14 ÷ 2 × 2 = ______

3. 382.4 × 0 + 5.3 = ______

4. 1 × 8.86 ÷ 1 = ______

5. 6.65 – 6.65 + 3.4 = ______

6. 8.04 × 1 – 8.04 = ______

11 Operations with Fractions

WORDS TO LEARN

Equivalent fractions – fractions that represent the same value

Simplest form – a fraction in which the numerator and denominator have only 1 as their common factor

$\frac{1}{2}$ and $\frac{2}{4}$ are equivalent fractions. $\frac{1}{2}$ is a fraction in simplest form.

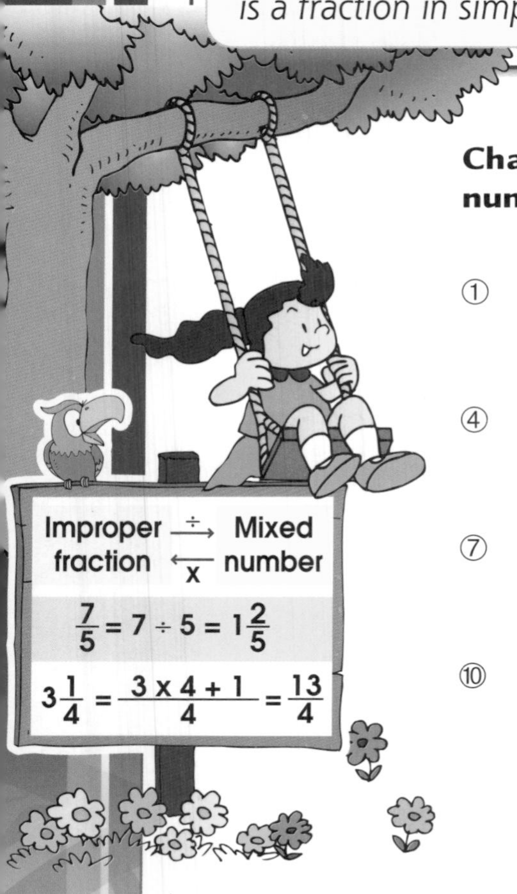

I am as strong as you.

$\frac{7}{5} = 7 \div 5 = 1\frac{2}{5}$
$3\frac{1}{4} = \frac{3 \times 4 + 1}{4} = \frac{13}{4}$

Change the improper fractions into mixed numbers or mixed numbers into improper fractions.

① $\frac{11}{3}$ = ______

② $4\frac{3}{7}$ = ______

③ $1\frac{4}{5}$ = ______

④ $2\frac{3}{5}$ = ______

⑤ $\frac{13}{9}$ = ______

⑥ $\frac{19}{6}$ = ______

⑦ $1\frac{3}{4}$ = ______

⑧ $\frac{18}{7}$ = ______

⑨ $3\frac{1}{8}$ = ______

⑩ $6\frac{1}{2}$ = ______

⑪ $2\frac{1}{2}$ = ______

⑫ $\frac{25}{9}$ = ______

Compare the fractions. Put '>' or '<' in the circles.

⑬ $\frac{5}{6}$ ◯ $\frac{7}{18}$

⑭ $\frac{4}{15}$ ◯ $\frac{2}{3}$

⑮ $2\frac{2}{5}$ ◯ $2\frac{7}{15}$

⑯ $5\frac{1}{2}$ ◯ $5\frac{3}{8}$

⑰ $\frac{9}{4}$ ◯ $2\frac{5}{8}$

⑱ $1\frac{1}{3}$ ◯ $\frac{11}{6}$

⑲ $1\frac{4}{7}$ ◯ $\frac{29}{21}$

⑳ $\frac{13}{9}$ ◯ $1\frac{1}{3}$

To compare fractions, find a common denominator and compare the numerators.
$\frac{8}{18} \rightarrow \frac{4}{9} > \frac{7}{18}$
Common denominator: 18

Add or subtract. Write the answers in simplest form.

21. 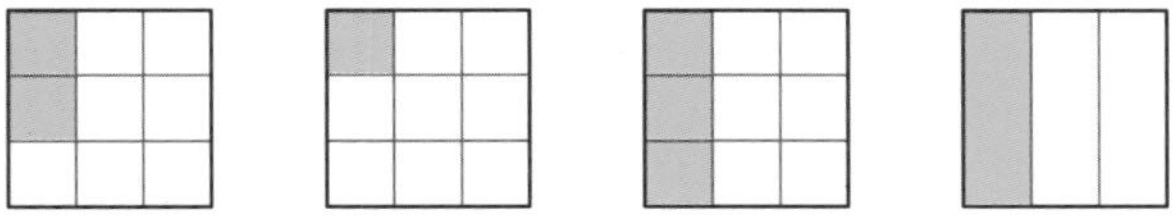

$\frac{2}{9} + \frac{1}{9} = \frac{\_\_\_}{9} = \frac{\_\_\_}{3}$

22. 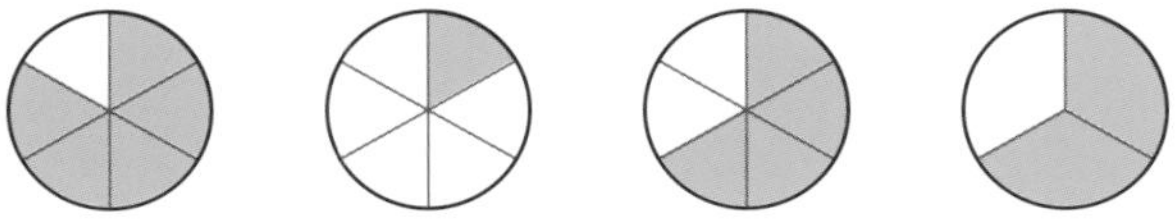

$\frac{5}{6} - \frac{1}{6} = \frac{\_\_\_}{6} = \frac{\_\_\_}{3}$

23. $\frac{11}{12} - \frac{5}{12} = \_\_\_\_ = \_\_\_\_$

24. $\frac{6}{7} + \frac{1}{7} = \_\_\_\_ = \_\_\_\_$

25. $\frac{8}{15} + \frac{2}{15} = \_\_\_\_ = \_\_\_\_$

26. $\frac{19}{20} - \frac{11}{20} = \_\_\_\_ = \_\_\_\_$

27. $\frac{3}{10} + \frac{9}{10} = \_\_\_\_ = \_\_\_\_$

28. $\frac{17}{18} - \frac{1}{18} = \_\_\_\_ = \_\_\_\_$

Solve the problems. Write the answers in simplest form.

29. The children spent $\frac{5}{12}$ h playing volleyball and $\frac{11}{12}$ h playing beach ball. How much time did the children spend playing ball games?

_______ h

30. Jason took $\frac{5}{8}$ h to pick 100 shells; Peter took $\frac{7}{8}$ h. How much longer did Peter take than Jason?

_______ h

31. $\frac{7}{15}$ of the children wore yellow T-shirts and $\frac{2}{15}$ of the children wore green T-shirts. What fraction of the children wore either yellow or green T-shirts?

_______ of the children

Look at the coloured parts of each diagram. Fill in the blanks with fractions to complete the addition or subtraction sentences.

32. 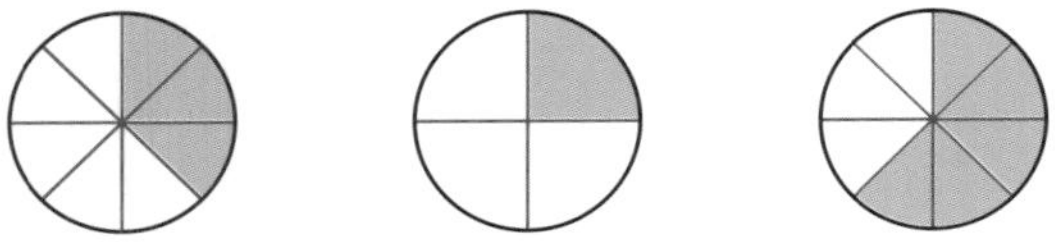

______ + ______ = ______

33. 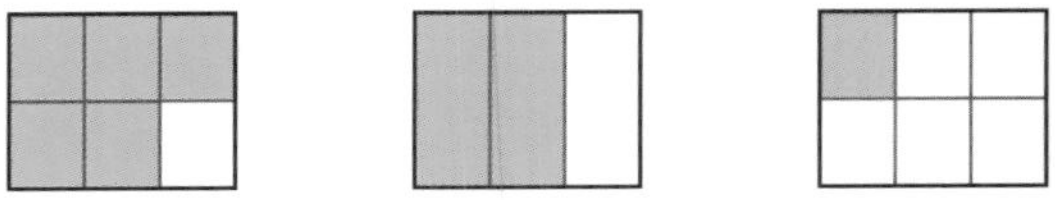

______ − ______ = ______

34. 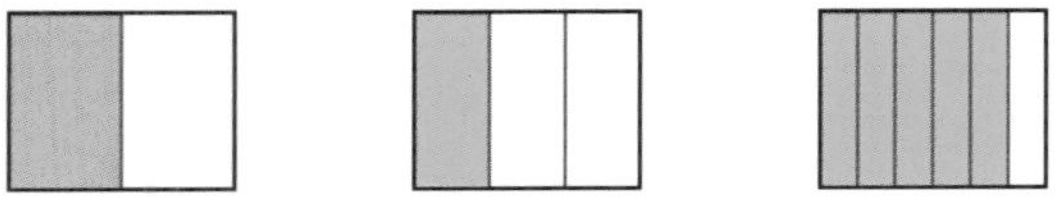

______ + ______ = ______

35. 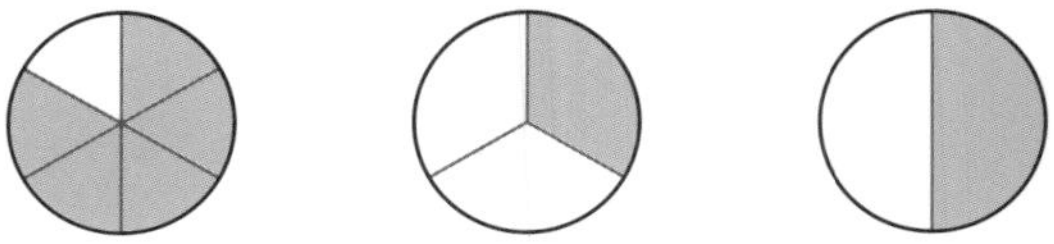

______ − ______ = ______

Write the answers in simplest form.

36. $\frac{2}{5} + \frac{1}{10}$

$= \frac{\quad}{10} + \frac{1}{10}$

$= \frac{\quad}{10}$

$=$ ______

37. $\frac{4}{7} - \frac{3}{14}$

$= \frac{\quad}{14} - \frac{3}{14}$

$= \frac{\quad}{14}$

To add/subtract fractions with different denominators:
• Write equivalent fractions with a common denominator.
• Add/subtract the numerators.
• Write the answer in simplest form.
$\frac{4}{15} + \frac{1}{3}$
Common denominator: 15
$= \frac{4}{15} + \frac{5}{15}$
$= \frac{9}{15}$ ← Add the numerators.
$= \frac{3}{5}$ ← Write the answer in simplest form.

38. $\frac{1}{3} + \frac{7}{24} =$ ______

39. $\frac{17}{20} - \frac{1}{5} =$ ______

40. $\frac{3}{4} + \frac{1}{12} =$ ______

41. $\frac{3}{5} - \frac{1}{3} =$ ______

42. $\frac{9}{10} - \frac{1}{2} =$ ______

43. $\frac{1}{15} + \frac{4}{5} =$ ______

44. $\frac{7}{16} - \frac{1}{4} =$ ______

45. $\frac{3}{4} + \frac{1}{20} =$ ______

46. $\frac{7}{8} - \frac{5}{16} =$ ______

47. $\frac{11}{24} - \frac{1}{3} =$ ______

Brian went camping with his family. Help him solve the problems. Write the answers in simplest form.

48. Brian and his family travelled $\frac{5}{6}$ h and walked $\frac{1}{3}$ h to get from their house to the camp site. How much time did they take in all?

They took ________ h in all.

49. Brian and his sister, Sara, went to get some water. If Brian carried $\frac{17}{20}$ pail of water and Sara carried $\frac{3}{4}$ pail of water, how much more water did Brian carry than Sara?

Brian carried ________ more pail of water than Sara.

50. Brian's father, Mr. Prem, took $\frac{9}{10}$ h to build the first tent and $\frac{1}{5}$ h to build the second tent. How much time did he spend building the tents?

He spent ________ h building the tents.

ACTIVITY

Solve the problem.

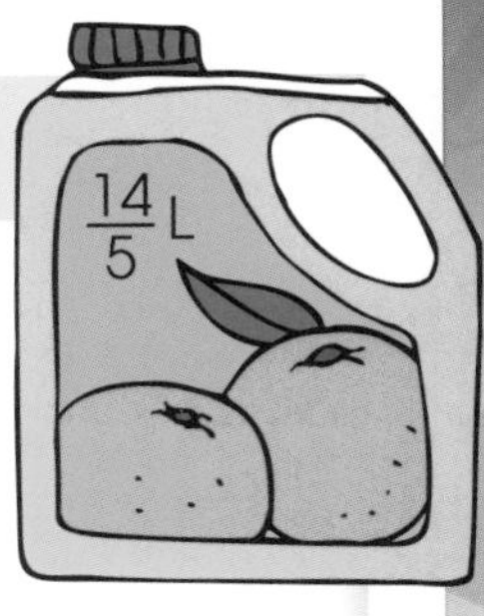

Brian has a jug of juice. If he drinks $\frac{2}{5}$ L every day, how many days will the jug of juice last?

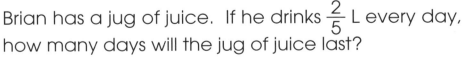

No. of Days	1	2		
Amount of Juice Consumed (L)	$\frac{2}{5}$	$\frac{4}{5}$		

The jug of juice will last ________ days.

12 Fractions, Decimals, and Percents

WORDS TO LEARN

Percent (%) – means a part of 100 or out of 100

e.g. 40% means 40 out of 100.

A percent $\xrightarrow{\div 100}$ **A fraction or decimal**

A fraction or decimal $\xrightarrow{\times 100}$ **A percent**

e.g. $57\% = 57 \div 100 = \frac{57}{100} = 0.57$

$\frac{29}{100} = \frac{29}{100} \times 100\% = 0.29 \times 100\% = 29\%$

About 30% of my bread has jam on it.

Rewrite as a percent (%).

① Twenty-five percent ________

② Fifty percent ________

③ 41 out of 100 ________

④ 7 out of 100 ________

⑤ 80 out of 100 ________

⑥ Two percent ________

⑦ Thirty percent ________

⑧ 92 out of 100 ________

Colour each 100-square grid to match each percent.

⑨
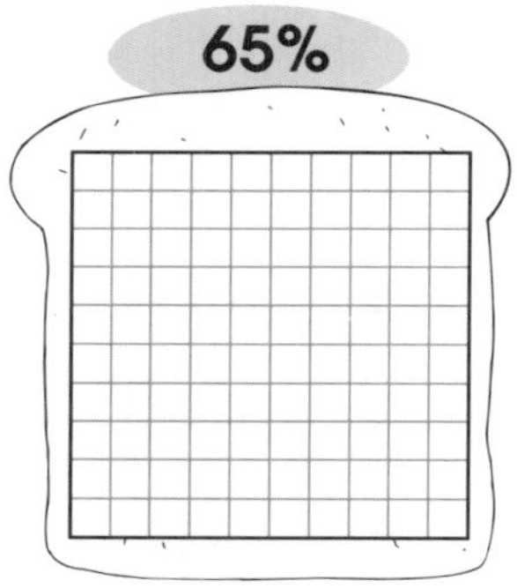

⑩
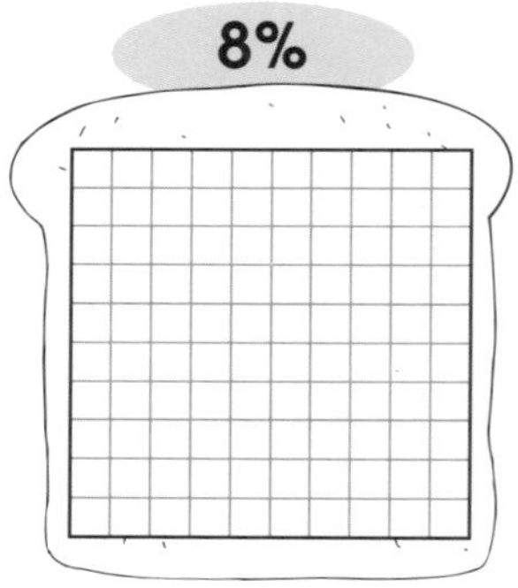

⑪
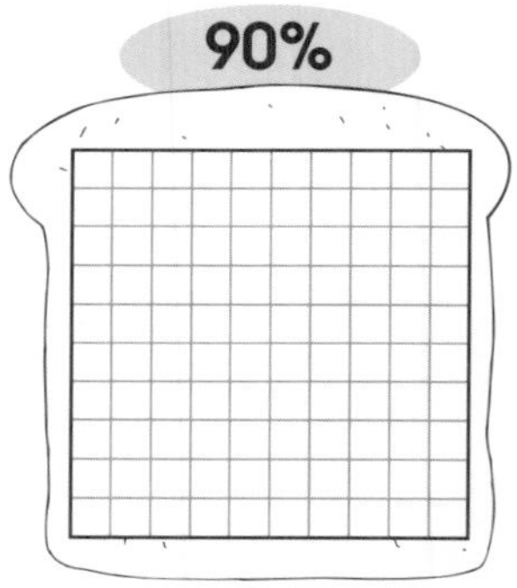

Write each coloured part as a fraction, decimal, and percent.

⑫
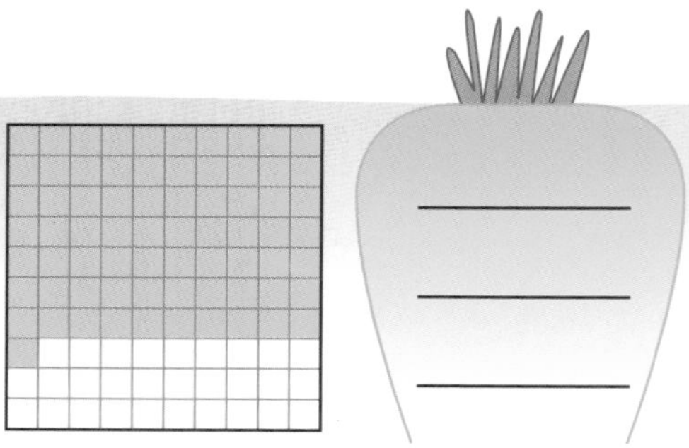

⑬
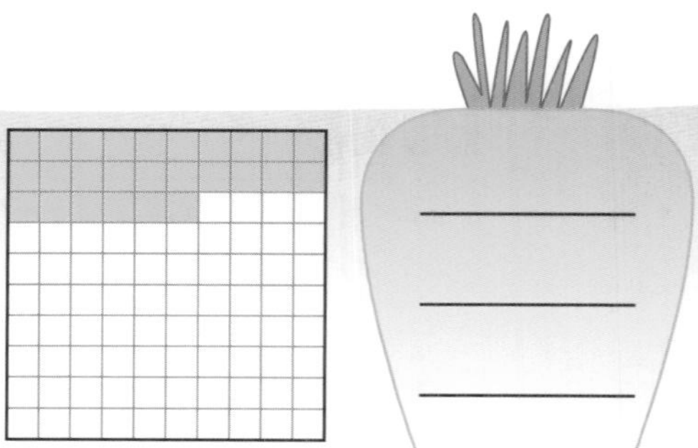

Rewrite as percents.

⑭ $\frac{13}{100}$ = ______ ⑮ $\frac{57}{100}$ = ______ ⑯ $\frac{8}{100}$ = ______

⑰ $\frac{7}{20}$ = $\frac{}{100}$ = ______ ⑱ $\frac{3}{4}$ = $\frac{}{100}$ = ______

⑲ $3\frac{8}{25}$ = $3\frac{}{100}$ = ______ ⑳ $4\frac{1}{2}$ = $4\frac{}{100}$ = ______

㉑ $1\frac{9}{10}$ = ______ = ______ ㉒ $\frac{11}{50}$ = ______ = ______

㉓ $2\frac{1}{4}$ = ______ = ______ ㉔ $1\frac{17}{20}$ = ______ = ______

Write a fraction as a percent:
2/5 = 40/100
= 40%
Write an equivalent fraction using 100 as the denominator.

Rewrite as fractions in simplest form.

㉕ 38% ______ ㉖ 60% ______ ㉗ 8% ______

㉘ 40% ______ ㉙ 190% ______ ㉚ 250% ______

Use the box graph to fill in the blanks.

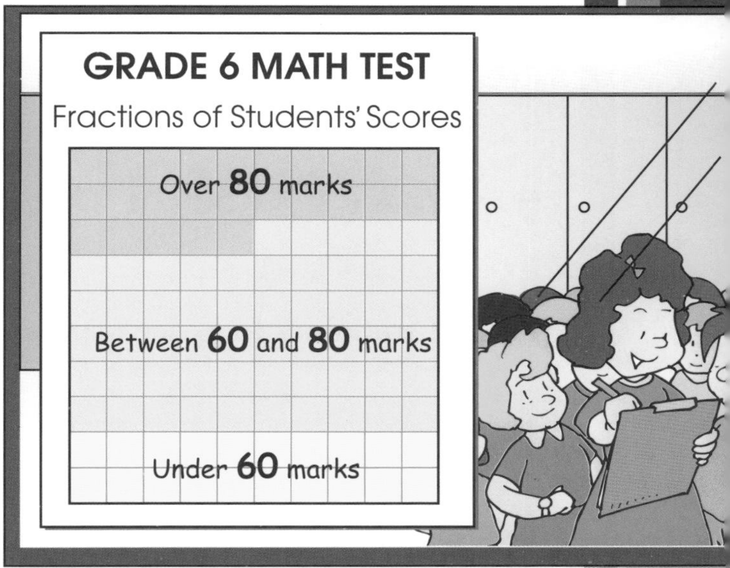

㉛ ______ % or ______ of the students got marks between 60 and 80.

㉜ ______ % or ______ of the students got more than 80 marks.

㉝ ______ % or ______ of the students got less than 60 marks.

㉞ There were 100 students;

a. ______ students got more than 80 marks.

b. ______ students got less than 60 marks.

c. ______ students got marks between 60 and 80.

Write the percents as fractions with 100 as the denominator first. Then write them as decimals.

165% = $\frac{165}{100}$
Write it as a mixed number.
= 1 $\frac{65}{100}$
= 1.65
x 100%
A decimal → A percent
e.g. 0.14 = 0.14 x 100%
= 14%

(35) 20% = $\frac{\quad}{100}$ = ______

(36) 5% = $\frac{\quad}{100}$ = ______

(37) 77% = ______ = ______

(38) 60% = ______ = ______

(39) 125% = ______ = ______

(40) 190% = ______ = ______

(41) 142% = ______ = ______

(42) 106% = ______ = ______

Write the decimals as percents.

(43) 0.34 = ______ %

(44) 0.06 = ______ %

(45) 0.8 = ______ %

(46) 1.43 = ______ %

(47) 1.2 = ______ %

(48) 0.27 = ______ %

(49) 6.04 = ______ %

(50) 0.92 = ______ %

Put '>' or '<' in the circles.

(51) 5.6% ◯ 0.56

(52) 24% ◯ 0.024

(53) 0.11 ◯ 10%

(54) 125% ◯ 1.52

(55) 3.08 ◯ 30.8%

(56) 42% ◯ 0.042

Put the numbers in order from smallest to greatest.

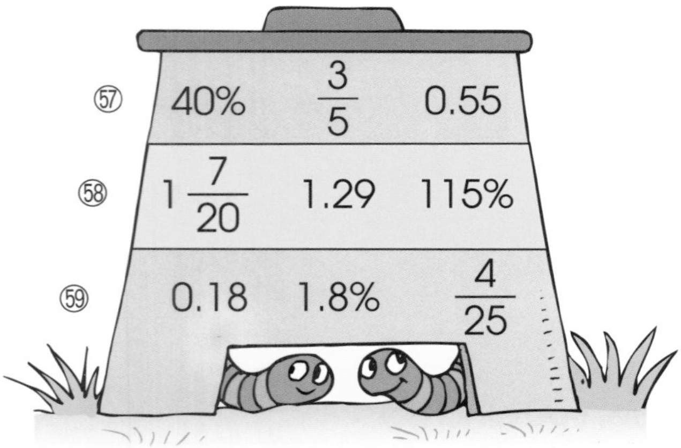

(57) 40% $\frac{3}{5}$ 0.55 ______________________

(58) $1\frac{7}{20}$ 1.29 115% ______________________

(59) 0.18 1.8% $\frac{4}{25}$ ______________________

Read what Uncle John says. Help him solve the problems.

There are 50 lightbulbs on a wire. 20 of them are red, 25 yellow, and the rest blue.

60. ________ (Fraction) or ________ (Percent) of the lightbulbs are red.

61. ________ (Percent) or ________ (Decimal) of the lightbulbs are yellow.

62. ________ (Fraction) or ________ (Decimal) of the lightbulbs are blue.

63. If 2 lightbulbs are burnt out, what percent of the lightbulbs are burnt out? ________

64. If 5 lightbulbs are removed, what percent of the lightbulbs are still on the wire? ________

Read the bar graph. Then answer the questions.

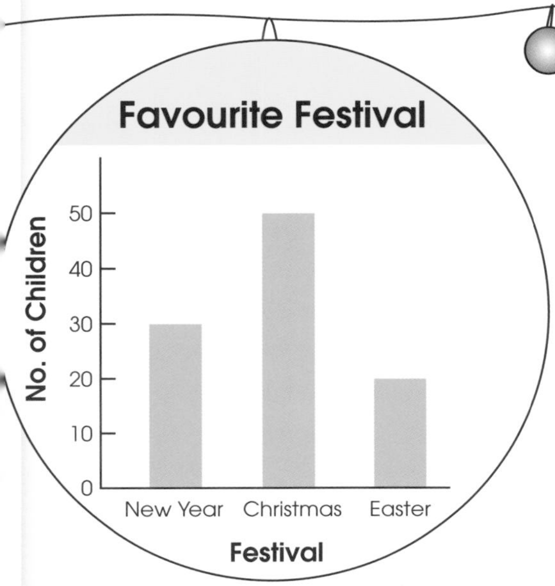

1. Which festival is the most popular?

   ____

2. If 100 children are asked about their favourite festivals, what percent of the children prefer

   a. New Year? ________

   b. Christmas? ________

   c. Easter? ________

13 Rate and Ratio

WORDS TO LEARN

Rate – a comparison of two numbers with different units
e.g. \$4/week, 100 km/h

Ratio – a comparison of numbers with the same unit
e.g. red apples to green apples = 3:4

A ratio can be expressed in fraction form, e.g. 3:4 = $\frac{3}{4}$.

Find the cost per kilogram of each kind of fruit.

①

 \$ ______ /kg

 \$ ______ /kg

 \$ ______ /kg

 \$ ______ /kg

 \$ ______ /kg

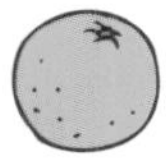 \$ ______ /kg

Which is the best buy in each group? Colour the correct answer.

② ③ ④

Look at the flying insects. Write the ratios.

2 boys
3 girls
boys to girls = 2:3
The no. of boys to the no. of girls is 2 to 3.

⑤ bees to butterflies = ____ : ____

⑥ dragonflies to butterflies = ________

⑦ dragonflies to bees = ________

⑧ bees to all = ________

⑨ dragonflies to all = ________

⑩ butterflies to all = ________

Follow the methods to write 2 equivalent ratios for each ratio.

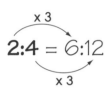

Multiply each term by 3.

x 3

2:4 = 6:12

x 3

Divide each term by 2.

÷ 2

2:4 = 1:2

÷ 2

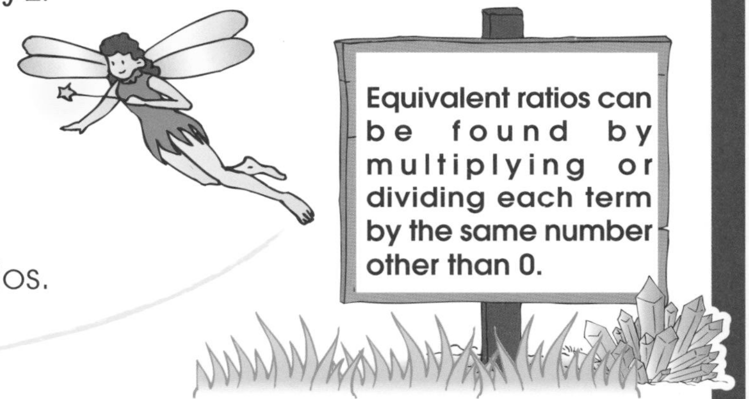

Equivalent ratios can be found by multiplying or dividing each term by the same number other than 0.

1:2, 2:4, and 6:12 are equivalent ratios.

⑪ 2:3 ________ ________

⑫ 5:4 ________ ________

⑬ 6:18 ________ ________

⑭ 8:6 ________ ________

⑮ 28:21 ________ ________

⑯ 4:10 ________ ________

The ratio is in simplest form if the only common factor of the terms is 1.
e.g. The ratio 3:2 is in simplest form.

Write each ratio in simplest form.

⑰ 5:10 ________

⑱ 12:32 ________

⑲ 8:14 ________

⑳ 9:6 ________

㉑ 12:20 ________

㉒ 15:20 ________

㉓ 24:3 ________

㉔ 18:8 ________

Look at the pictures that Sam has drawn. Help him write each ratio in simplest form.

㉕

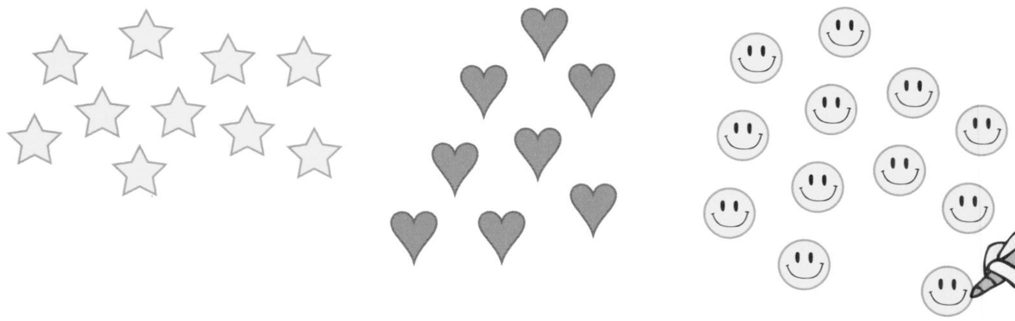

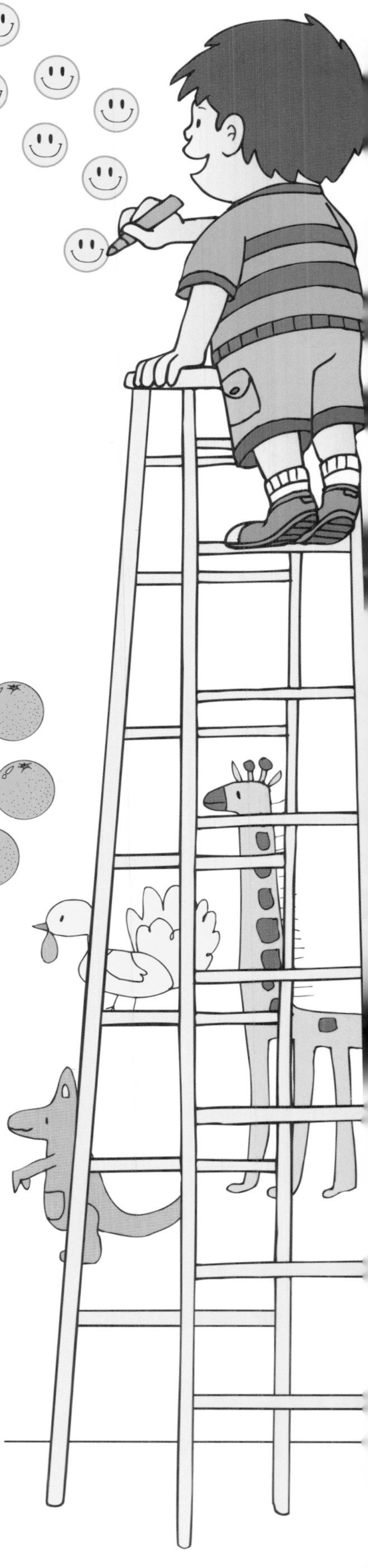

a. stars to happy faces = ________

b. hearts to happy faces = ________

c. happy faces to all = ________

d. hearts to all = ________

e. stars to all = ________

㉖

a. apples to oranges = ________

b. oranges to pears = ________

c. apples to pears = ________

d. red apples to green apples = ________

e. yellow pears to green pears = ________

f. small oranges to big oranges = ________

g. green apples to green pears = ________

h. pears to all = ________

i. oranges to all = ________

Today is Mr. Beth's birthday. His grandchildren are celebrating with him. Help the children solve the problems. Write the answers in simplest form.

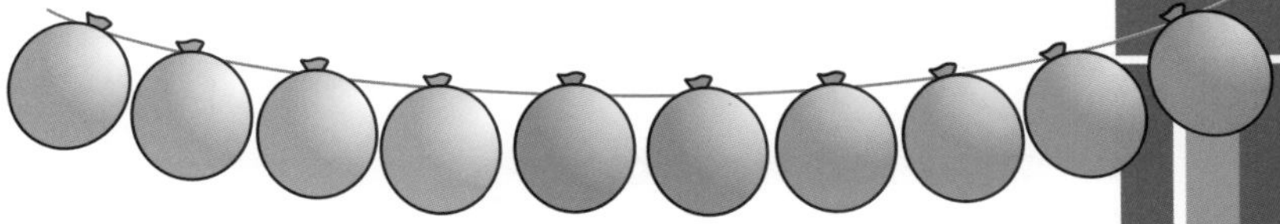

(27) What is the ratio of red balloons to blue balloons?

____

(28) What is the ratio of green balloons to red balloons?

____

(29) What is the ratio of grandsons to granddaughters?

____

(30) What is the ratio of orange juice to apple juice? __________

(31) What is the unit price of a box of orange juice? __________

(32) What is the unit price of a box of apple juice? __________

(33) What is the cost per kilogram for the birthday cake? __________

ACTIVITY

Answer the questions. Write the ratios in simplest form.

① What is the ratio of the free balloons to the paid balloons? __________

② If Louis buys 30 balloons, how many free balloons will he get? __________

③ There are 16 balloons in a bag. What is the ratio of paid balloons to free balloons in that bag? __________

14 Patterns and Simple Equations

WORDS TO LEARN

Pattern rule – a rule that describes a pattern

e.g. 1 $\xrightarrow{\times 2 + 1}$ 3 $\xrightarrow{\times 2 + 1}$ 7 $\xrightarrow{\times 2 + 1}$ 15 $\xrightarrow{\times 2 + 1}$ 31 . . . The pattern rule is double the previous term and add 1.

Equation – a mathematical statement having equivalent terms on either side of the equal sign

Think :  + 10 = 95

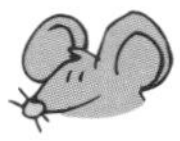 = 85

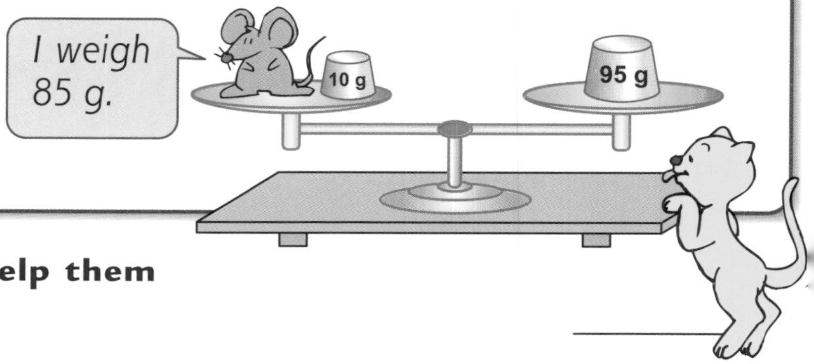

Read what the animals say. Help them complete the number patterns.

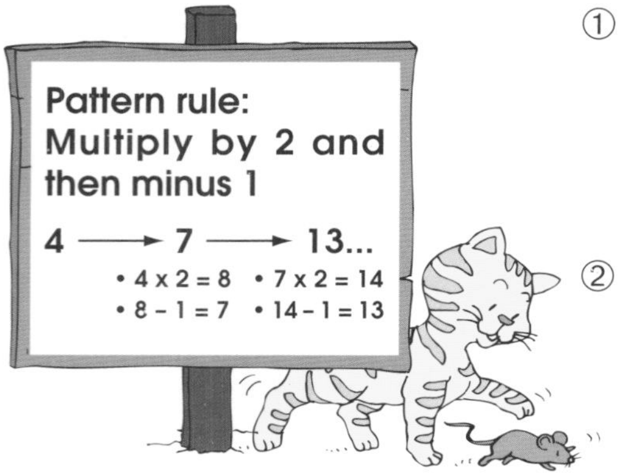

Pattern rule:
Multiply by 2 and then minus 1
4 → 7 → 13...
• 4 x 2 = 8 • 7 x 2 = 14
• 8 – 1 = 7 • 14 – 1 = 13

① *Multiply by 3 and then plus 1.*

3 ____ ____ ____ ____ ____

② *Subtract 2 and then multiply by 2.*

12 ____ ____ ____ ____ ____

Look for the patterns. Describe the rules and extend the patterns.

③ 2 3 6 15 42

Pattern rule: ______________________________

④ 8 17 35 71 143

Pattern rule: ______________________________

⑤ 532 276 148 84 52

Pattern rule: ______________________________

The aliens have recorded their heights. Help them complete the graph to show the pattern of their heights. Then answer the questions.

⑥

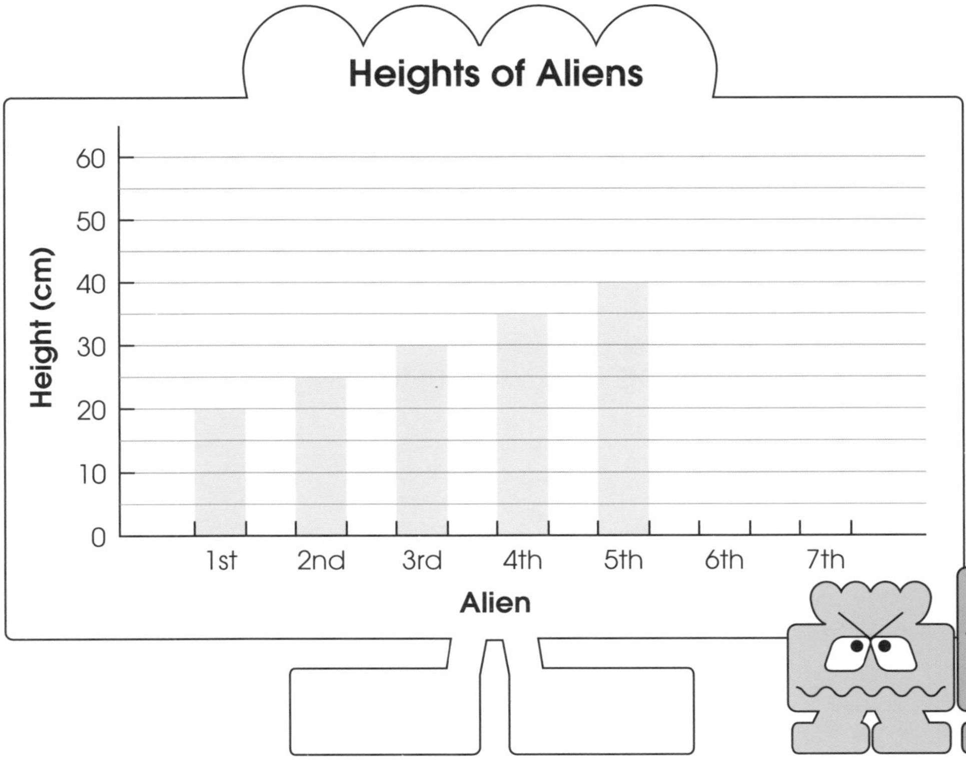

⑦ What is the height of the 7th alien? ____________

⑧ Which alien is 35 cm in height? ____________

⑨ Which alien is 10 cm taller than the 3rd alien? ____________

⑩ How tall is the 9th alien? ____________

⑪ Describe the pattern of the heights of the aliens.

____

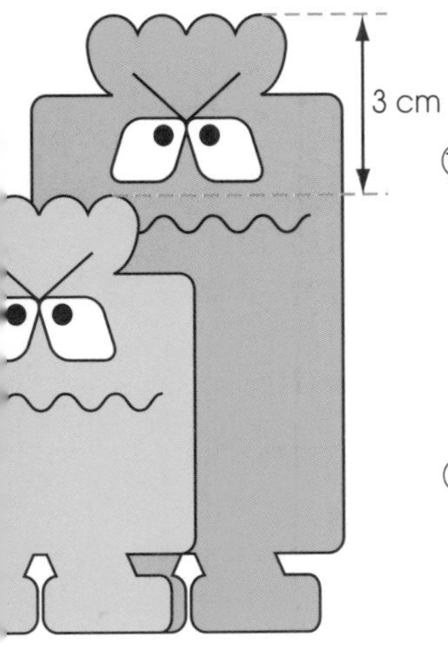

If each alien has grown by 3 cm, complete the table to show their new heights. Then answer the question.

⑫ The new heights of aliens:

Alien	1st	2nd	3rd	4th	5th	6th	7th
New Height (cm)							

⑬ Do the new heights of the aliens follow a pattern? If so, what pattern do they follow?

____

The children are in a wax museum. The data in each table follows a pattern. Help them complete the tables and answer the questions.

⑭ Number of wax figures:

a.

Year	2002	2003	2004	2005		
No. of Wax Figures	145	170	195	220		

b. How many wax figures will there be by 2008?

_________ wax figures

c. In which year will there be 345 wax figures in the museum?

____

⑮ Number of visitors:

a.

Year	Jul	Aug	Sep	Oct		
No. of Visitors	1800	2000	2300	2700		

b. How many people will visit the museum in January next year?

_________ people

c. In which month next year will 7200 people visit the museum?

____

Find the unknown in each equation.

⑯  $- 8 = 2$

 = _______

⑰ $6 +$ 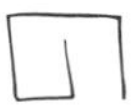 $= 9$

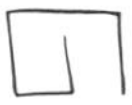 = _______

⑱ $6 \times$ 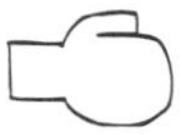 $= 30$

 = _______

⑲ 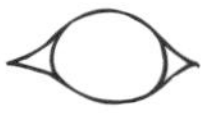 $\div 2 = 3$

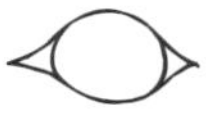 = _______

⑳ 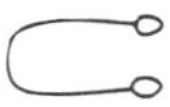 $+ 9 = 17$

 = _______

㉑  $\times 4 = 28$

 = _______

Use 'Guess-and-Test' method to find the unknown.
e.g. 6 + = 10
Guess | = 3 | = 4
Test | 6 + 3 = 9 | 6 + 4 = 10
= 4

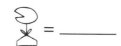

Write an equation for each statement. Then find the unknown.

㉒ 6 more than a number y is 11.

The number is ________ .

㉓ 2 times a number c is 8.

The number is ________ .

㉔ 8 less than a number k is 20.

The number is ________ .

㉕ A number b divided by 9 is 5.

The number is ________ .

㉖ 5 plus a number m is 17.

The number is ________ .

㉗ A number g times 4 is 32.

The number is ________ .

㉘ Take away 3 from a number u is 4.

The number is ________ .

㉙ A number a multiplied by 6 is 24.

The number is ________ .

ACTIVITY

Write a mathematical expression for each statement and answer the question.

Brother Worm is y cm long.

① Sister Worm is 3 times as long as Brother Worm. ________

② Cousin Worm is 4 cm longer than Brother Worm. ________

③ Baby Worm is 2 cm shorter than Sister Worm. ________

④ Who is the longest? ________

15 Transformations and Coordinates

WORDS TO LEARN

Transformation – a change in a figure resulting in a different position or orientation
Transformations include the translation (slide), reflection (flip), and rotation (turn).

Coordinates – an ordered pair used to describe a location on a grid
The order of a pair is expressed as (units across, units up).

The green triangle is the translated image of the red triangle. It is 2 units up and 3 units left from the red one.

The coordinates of the vertices of the green triangle are (3,4), (4,2) and (2,2).

Draw the images of the shapes. Then answer the questions.

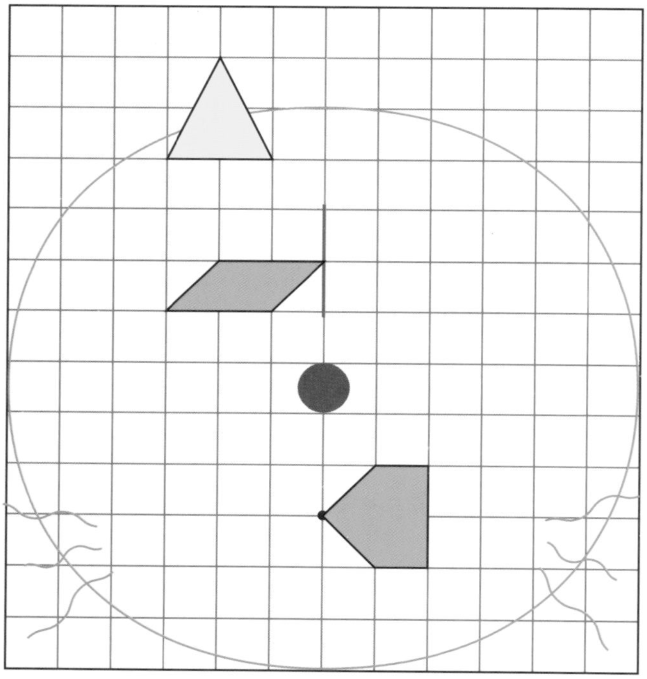

① a. Translate the triangle 1 unit down and 5 units right and colour it pink.

b. Flip the parallelogram over the green line and colour it blue.

c. Rotate the pentagon a half turn about • and colour it purple.

② Do the parallelograms have the same area?

____

③ If the area of the yellow triangle is 2 square units, what is the area of the pink triangle? __________

④ If the coordinates of the turn centre are (6,3), what are the coordinates of the vertices of the purple pentagon?

____

Read what Frankie the Farmer says. Help him plot his field on the grid and find out the missing vertex. Then answer the questions.

I have a field in the shape of a parallelogram. The coordinates of three vertices of my field are (1,0), (2,3), and (6,3). What are the coordinates of the 4th vertex?

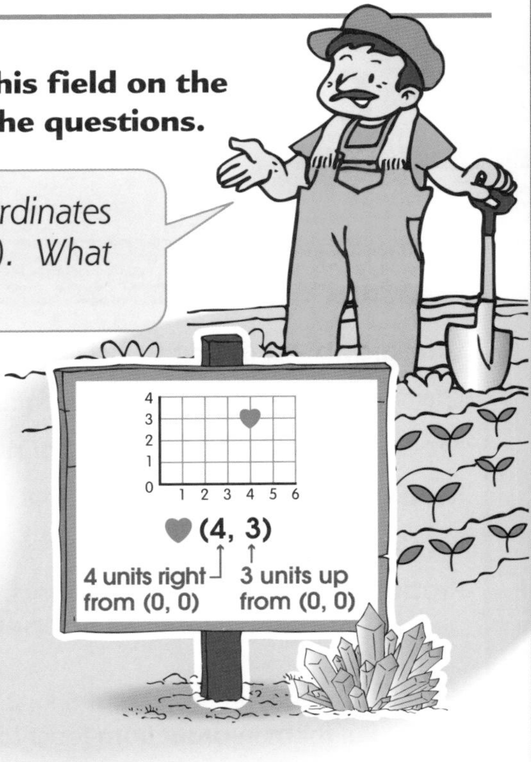

⑤

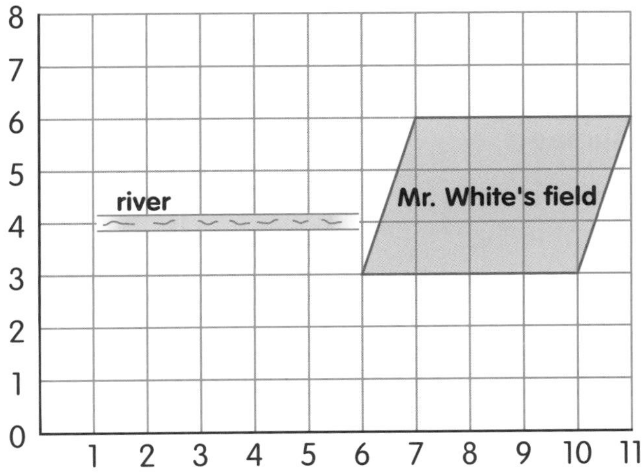

The coordinates of the 4th vertex are ________ .

⑥ The area of Frankie's field is ________ square units.

⑦ If you reflect Frankie's field over the river, you can find Mr. Beth's field. Draw the reflected image. Then write the coordinates of the vertices of Mr. Beth's field.

____

⑧ What transformation can you do to Frankie's field so that Mr. White's field is its transformed image? Describe the transformation.

____

ACTIVITY

Draw the line of reflection.

The brown figure is the reflected image of the yellow one.

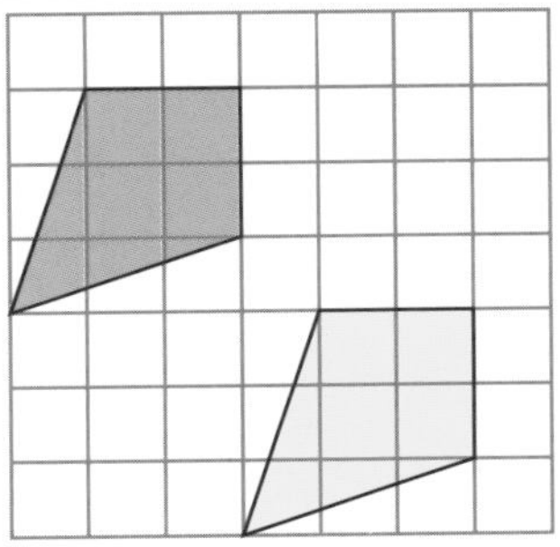

16 Graphs and Probability

WORDS TO LEARN

Line graph – a graph using lines or points to show information 

Circle graph – using parts in a circle to show information about a whole 

Mean – the average of a set of numbers

Median – the middle number of a set of numbers

Mode – the number in a set which occurs most often

Probability – a number showing how likely it is that an event will happen

Numbers on the cards: 8, 6, 2, 8
Put them in order from least to greatest: 2, 6, 8, 8
Mean: $(2 + 6 + 8 + 8) \div 4 = 6$
Mode: 8
Median: $(6 + 8) \div 2 = 7$

Judy has 4 cards. She lets me pick one.
8 6 2 8
The probability of picking a 2 is $\frac{1}{4}$.

See how many blocks Joseph has. Help him complete the table. Then use a bar graph and a circle graph to show the data and answer the questions.

①

Colour	Green	Purple	Red
No. of Blocks	4		
Fraction of the Whole	$\frac{1}{4}$		

②

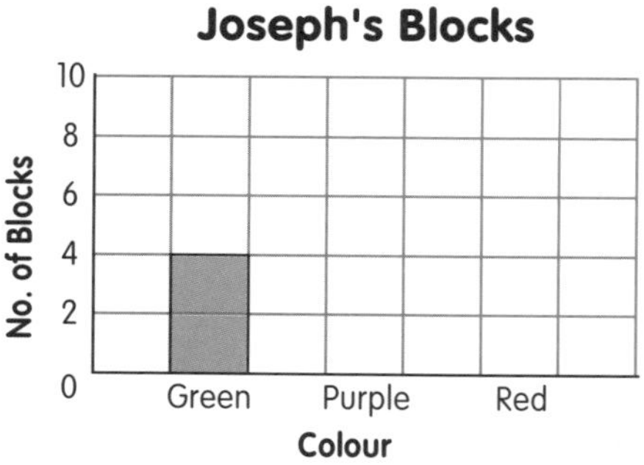

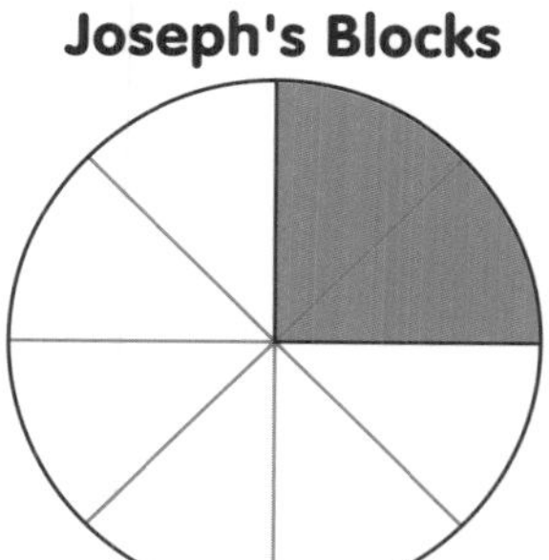

③ Joseph wants to know what fraction of the blocks are red. Which graph should he refer to? ____________

④ Joseph wants to know how many more red blocks than purple blocks he has. Which graph should he refer to? ____________

Use a line graph to show the number of sandwiches sold in the past few days. Then answer the questions.

Day	Number of Tuna Sandwiches Sold	Number of Chicken Sandwiches Sold
SUN	75	80
MON	50	10
TUE	30	25
WED	40	40
THU	50	55

⑤

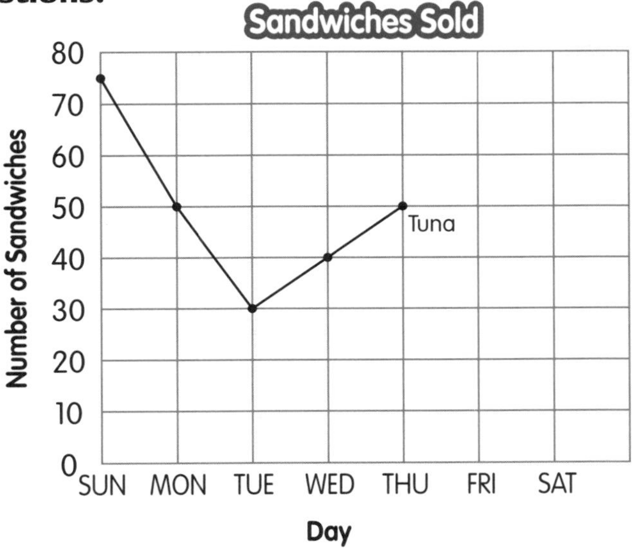

⑥ The mean of tuna sandwiches sold is ____________ .

⑦ The median of chicken sandwiches sold is ____________ .

⑧ The mode of tuna sandwiches sold is ____________ .

⑨ Follow the trends to find how many chicken sandwiches and tuna sandwiches will be sold on Saturday.

____________ chicken sandwiches; ____________ tuna sandwiches

Put each set of data in order from least to greatest. Then find its mean, median, and mode.

⑩ 64 cups 24 cups 73 cups 64 cups 24 cups 70 cups 24 cups

____

Mean: ________
Median: ________
Mode: ________

⑪ 21 bags 15 bags 18 bags 18 bags 15 bags 15 bags

____

Mean: ________
Median: ________
Mode: ________

16

Johnny the Monkey is going to pick an apple. Write the probability in fractions in simplest form. Then colour the circle graph to match the probability.

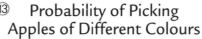

⑫ The probability of picking

a. a green apple

____

b. a red apple

____

c. a golden apple

____

⑬ Probability of Picking Apples of Different Colours

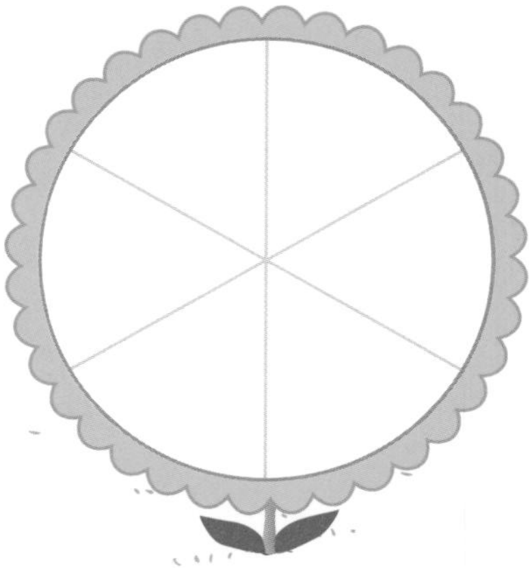

Colour the pictures to match each situation.

⑭

The probability of picking a yellow mushroom is $\frac{3}{8}$.

The probability of picking a red mushroom is $\frac{1}{2}$.

The probability of picking a purple mushroom is $\frac{1}{8}$.

⑮ The probability of picking a red flower is $\frac{2}{5}$.

The probability of picking a yellow flower is $\frac{1}{2}$.

The probability of picking a purple flower is $\frac{1}{10}$.

The girls want to buy some chips. Help them complete the tree diagram to show all the choices. Answer the questions.

⑯ **Brand** **Packaging** **Flavour**

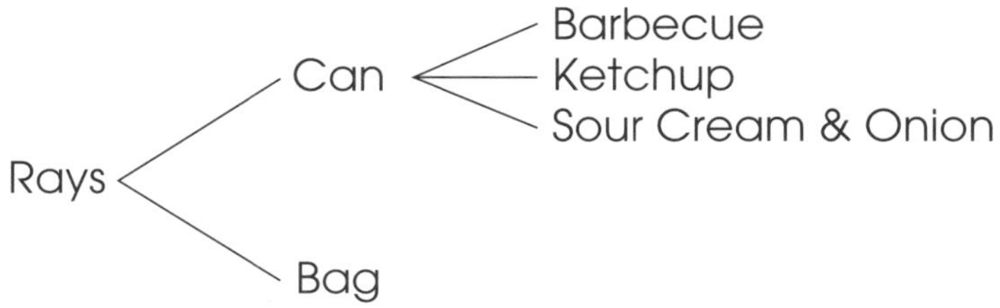

⑰ How many choices are there in all? ________

⑱ How many choices are there in Ray's products? ________

⑲ How many choices are with ketchup flavour? ________

⑳ What is the probability of a customer choosing

a. a bag of barbecue-flavoured chips? ________

b. a can of chips? ________

ACTIVITY

Answer the questions.

① When a coin is tossed 3 times, the probability of getting 2H and 1T is ________ .

② When a coin is tossed 4 times, the probability of getting 3H and 1T is ________ .

Final Test

Rewrite as percents. (4 marks)

① $\frac{7}{10}$ = ________

② $9\frac{1}{4}$ = ________

③ 2.83 = ________

④ 0.17 = ________

Find the answers. (7 marks)

⑤ $\begin{array}{r} 8.239 \\ +\ 1.678 \\ \hline \end{array}$

⑥ $\begin{array}{r} 6.009 \\ -\ 3.773 \\ \hline \end{array}$

⑦ $\begin{array}{r} 7.287 \\ \times\ \ \ \ \ 6 \\ \hline \end{array}$

⑧ $6.986 \div 7$ = ________

⑨ 3.4×1.9 = ________

⑩ $9.4 \div 0.2$ = ________

⑪ 8.2×1.6 = ________

Solve the problems. (6 marks)

⑫ Find the volume of each solid.

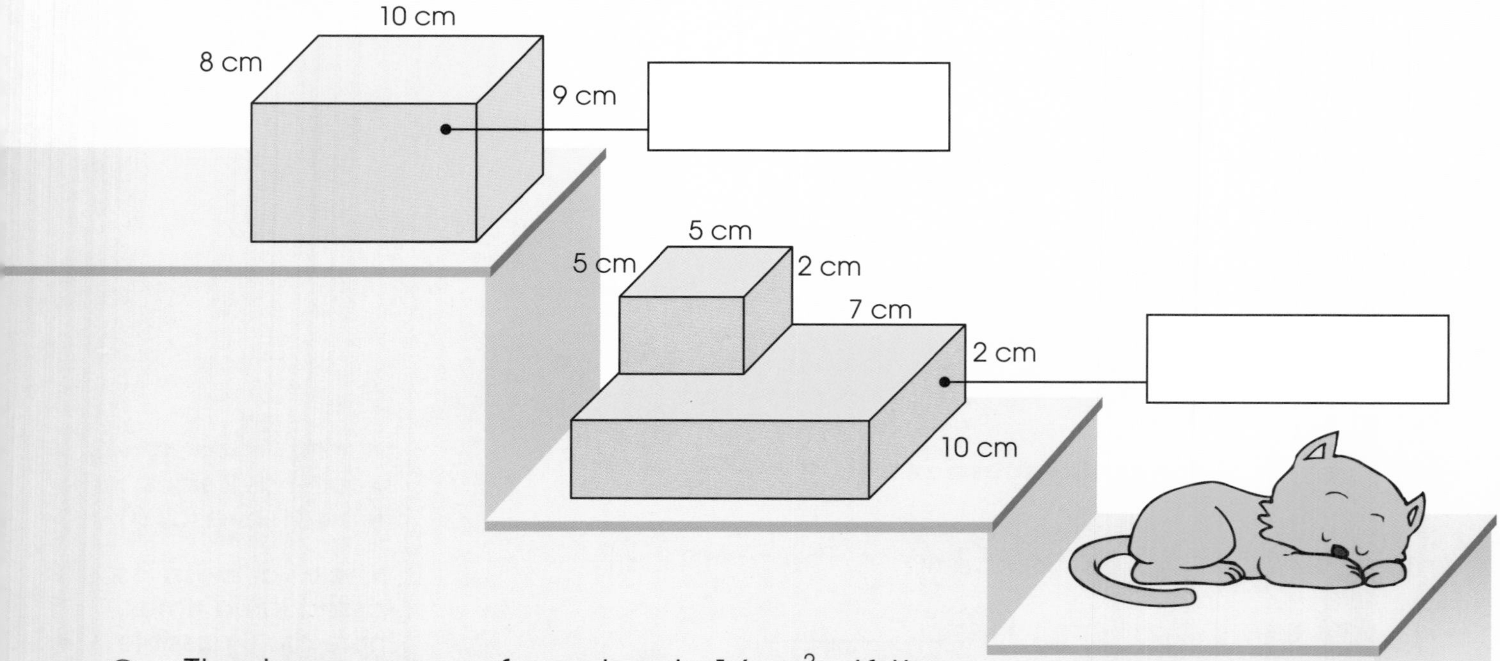

⑬ The base area of a prism is 16 m^2. If the height of the prism is 8 m, what is its volume?

____

Look at the picture. Write each ratio in simplest form. (8 marks)

⑭ boys to girls

____

⑮ boys to all children

____

⑯ girls wearing pants to girls wearing skirts

____

⑰ children having blonde hair to children having dark hair

____

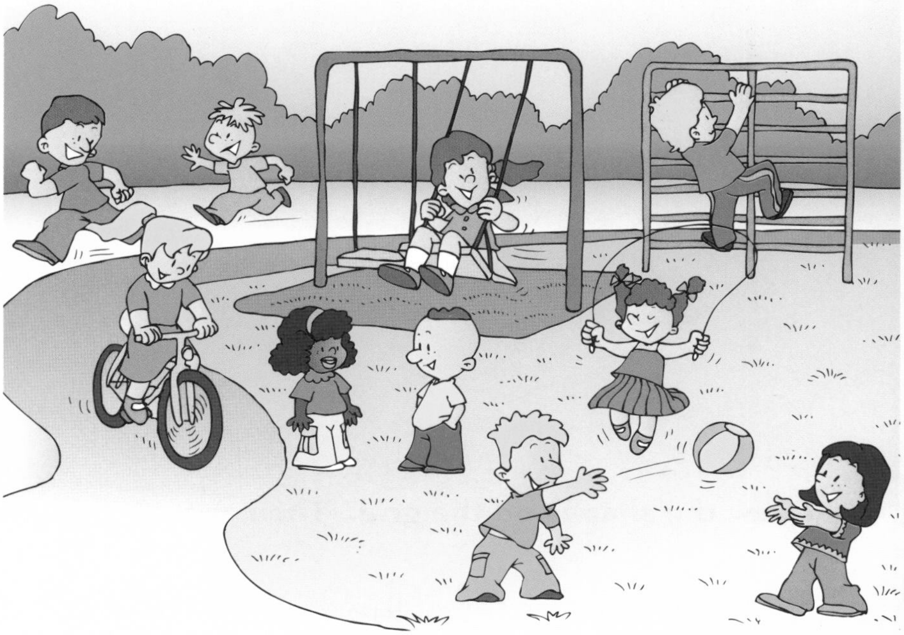

Write an equivalent ratio for each ratio. (4 marks)

⑱ 3:7 ______________

⑲ 12:6 ______________

⑳ 18:24 ______________

㉑ 9:4 ______________

Draw pictures on the spinner to match the probabilities. Then write a fraction in simplest form to complete the sentence. (4 marks)

㉒

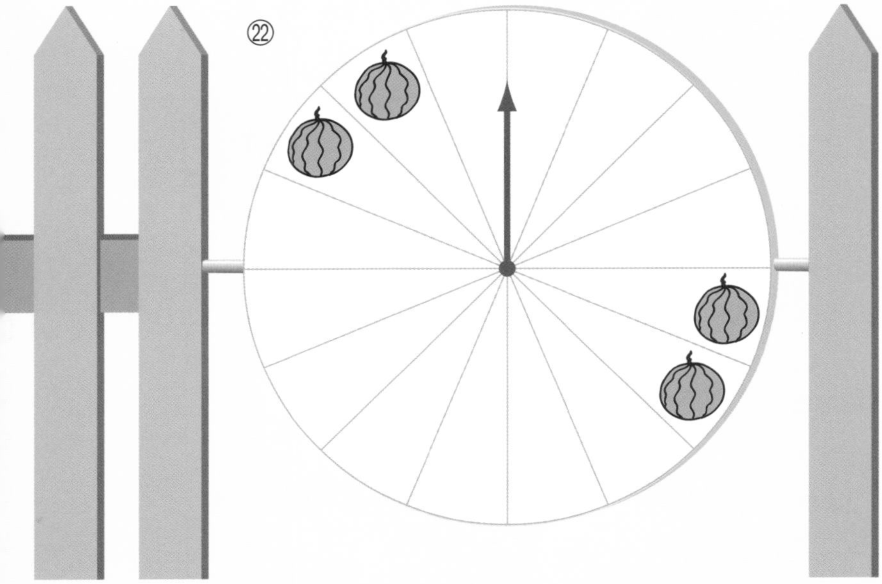

The probability of spinning on

- '  ' – $\frac{1}{4}$
- '  ' – $\frac{3}{8}$
- '  ' – $\frac{1}{8}$

㉓ The probability of spinning on  is __________ .

Final Test

Find the answers. Show your work. Write the answers in simplest form. (8 marks)

㉔ $\frac{5}{9} + \frac{1}{9} =$

㉕ $\frac{11}{12} - \frac{5}{12} =$

㉖ $\frac{2}{3} - \frac{1}{6} =$

㉗ $\frac{3}{10} + \frac{1}{2} =$

Draw the shapes on the grid. Then answer the questions. (8 marks)

㉘ The coordinates of the vertices of a quadrilateral are (1,7), (3,7), (3,5), and (1,4). Plot it on the grid and colour it yellow.

㉙ Reflect the quadrilateral over the green line and colour it blue.

㉚ Rotate the blue shape $\frac{1}{4}$ counterclockwise turn about (7,4) and colour it orange.

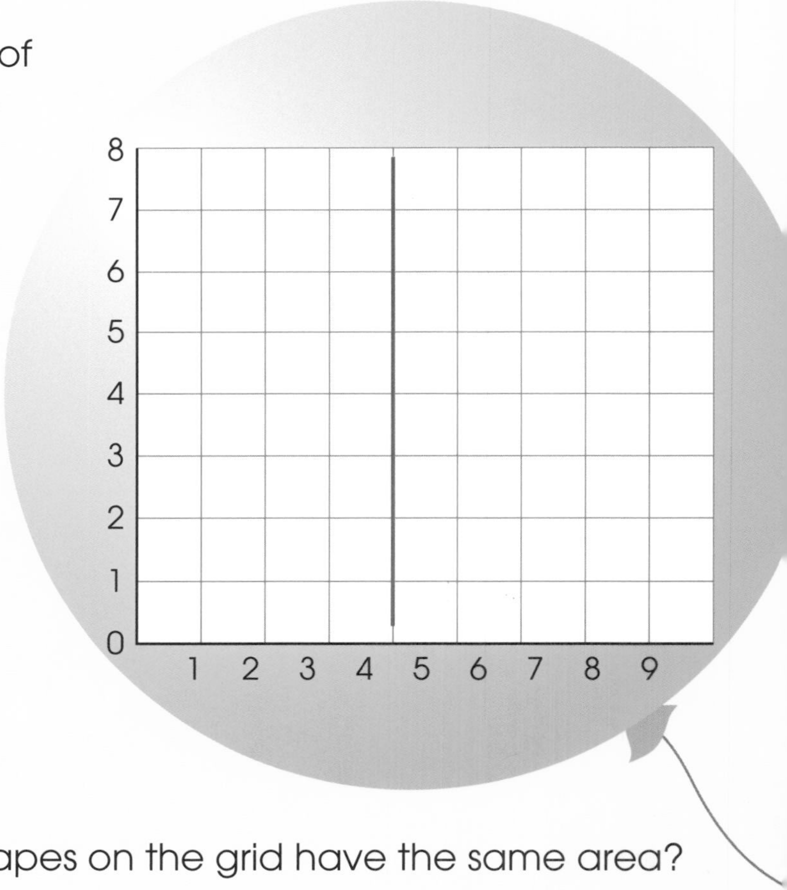

㉛ Do the shapes on the grid have the same area?

____

Look at the picture. Find the unit price of each item. (4 marks)

Unit Price

32  .... $

33  .... $

34  .... $

35  .... $

Help the children solve the problems. (10 marks)

36 Judy can run 28.98 m in 9 s. What is her speed?

____

37 Kevin runs at a speed of 2.94 m/s for 6 s. What is the distance covered by him?

____

38 Leo runs at a speed of 3.14 m/s for 3 s and 2.85 m/s for 8 s. What is the total distance covered by him?

____

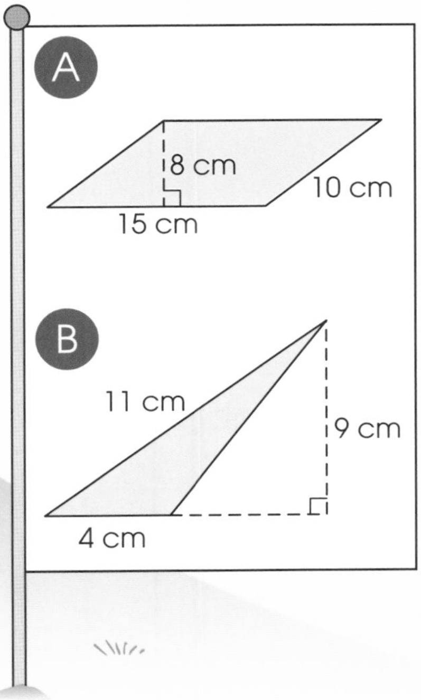

39 What is the area of each shape on the flag?

A : ________________ B : ________________

Final Test

Complete the tree diagram to show all kinds of new books. Then answer the questions. (9 marks)

⑩

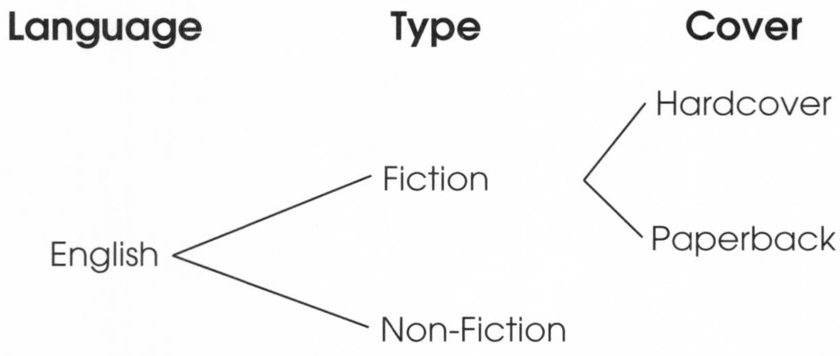

㊶ How many kinds of books are there? ____________

㊷ How many kinds of books are in French? ____________

㊸ What is the probability of a child choosing

a. a hardcover English fiction? ____________

b. a Spanish fiction? ____________

c. a paperback? ____________

Write an equation for each statement. Then find the unknown. (4 marks)

㊹ A number k divided by 5 is 7.

㊺ The sum of a number p and 8 is 24.

Alex the Alien is travelling from Planet A to Planet B. The times in the table follow a pattern. Help Alex complete the table and answer the questions. (4 marks)

46 a. Distance from Planet A

Time	9:00 a.m.	9:15 a.m.	9:30 a.m.	9:45 a.m.	10:00 a.m.	10:15 a.m.
Distance (km)	8.5	16	23.5	31		

b. At what time will Alex be 61 km from Planet A?

____

c. What will be the distance between Alex and Planet A at 11:15 a.m.?

____

Make a line graph to show how many aliens visited Planet A or Planet B in the past few days. Then answer the questions. (6 marks)

Alien Visitors

Day	Planet A	Planet B
SUN	95	15
MON	20	35
TUE	50	50
WED	60	50
THU	70	50

47

Aliens Visiting the Planets

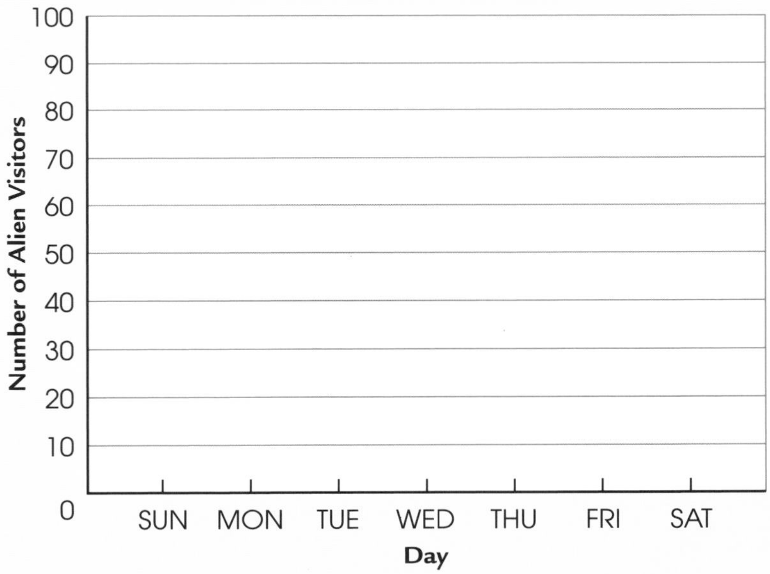

48 Find the mean of alien visitors to Planet A. __________

49 Find the median of alien visitors to Planet B. __________

50 Describe the number of aliens visiting Planet B in the past five days.

____

Final Test

Find the weight of each bag of candies. Then find the mean and median weight of the group. (5 marks)

51 a.

________ g

b.

________ g

c.

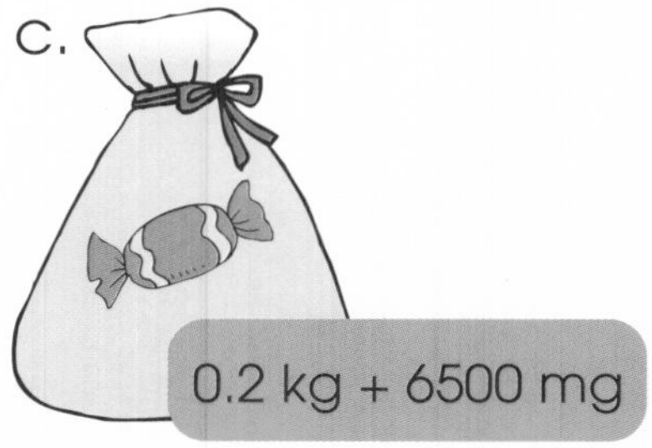

________ g

52 The mean weight is ________ g.

53 The median weight is ________ g.

Help Amy solve the problems. (9 marks)

54 What is the ratio of stars to the total number of shapes?

55 Amy completed part of her journey in $\frac{4}{5}$ h and the remainder in $\frac{1}{2}$ h. How long did she take to complete the whole journey?

56 Amy wants to buy her dog a sausage. If 12 sausages cost $4.08, how much does Amy need to pay for the sausage?

Score

100

Assessment Test 1

Mrs. Martin is asking her students where they want to go for the next outing. Look at the record. Help her complete the circle graph to show the information. Then answer the questions.

	Boys	Girls
Science Centre	5	1
Art Museum	2	2
Adventure Place	4	10

①

Each sector represents 2 children. Remember to label each sector in the circle graph.

② For the children who like going to Adventure Place, what is the ratio of boys to girls?

____

Find out the number of boys and girls in the class first.

③ What is the ratio of girls to boys in Mrs. Martin's class?

____

④ Mrs. Martin says, 'More than 50% of my students want to go to Adventure Place.' Is she correct? Explain.

____

____

Mrs. Martin is ordering on-line tickets for the students. Look at the screen. Answer the questions.

Adventure Place
• Tickets are only $23.55 per person including all taxes.
• Purchase 7 tickets and the 8th is free.
• Free admission for teachers and bus drivers.
• Adventure Place will provide badges for identification purposes.

⑤ 24 students are going to Adventure Place. How many tickets does Mrs. Martin need to order? Show your work.

For every 8 students, only 7 tickets are needed.

She needs to order ________ tickets.

⑥ What is the cost of the tickets ordered?

$ ________

⑦ Mrs. Martin will put the children into groups. If each group has the same number of children and there are no more than 5 groups, how can the children be divided? How many students are in each group? Show your work.

For question ⑦, think about the factors of 24. They are 1, 2, 3, 4, 6,...

Look at the badges provided. Help the children draw lines on the badges to complete the symmetrical shapes.

⑧

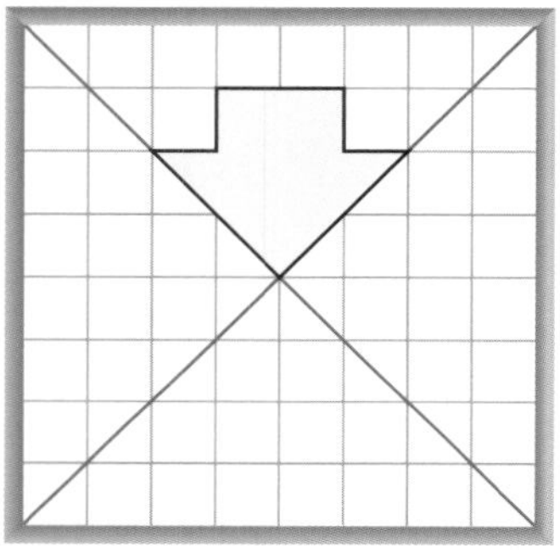

⑨

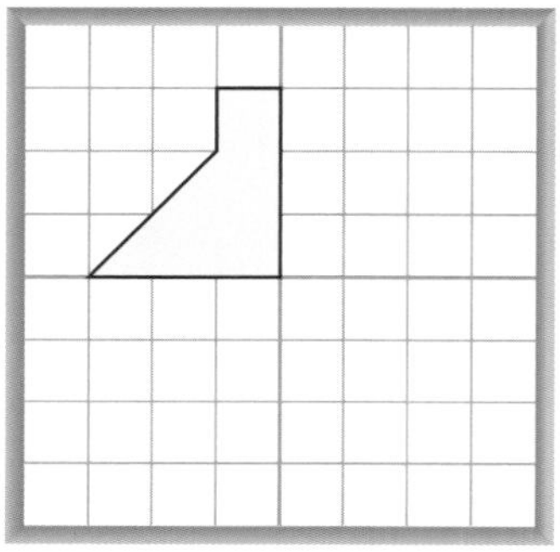

Leona and Tiffany are excited about the trip to the Adventure Place. Look at the notice. Help them answer the questions.

A Trip to Adventure Place

Date of Visit: June ▭ — A prime number between 24 and 34

Time: 8:00 – ▭ — 5 hours after noon

Things needed:

1. A piece of paper in the shape of a parallelogram with an area of 3000 cm².
2. Crayons in multiples of 3.

⑩ What is the date for the visit?

____

⑪ At what time will the activity finish? (Use 24-h clock time to show the time.)

____

⑫ How long will the activity last?

____

⑬ Draw a possible shape of the piece of paper that the students need.

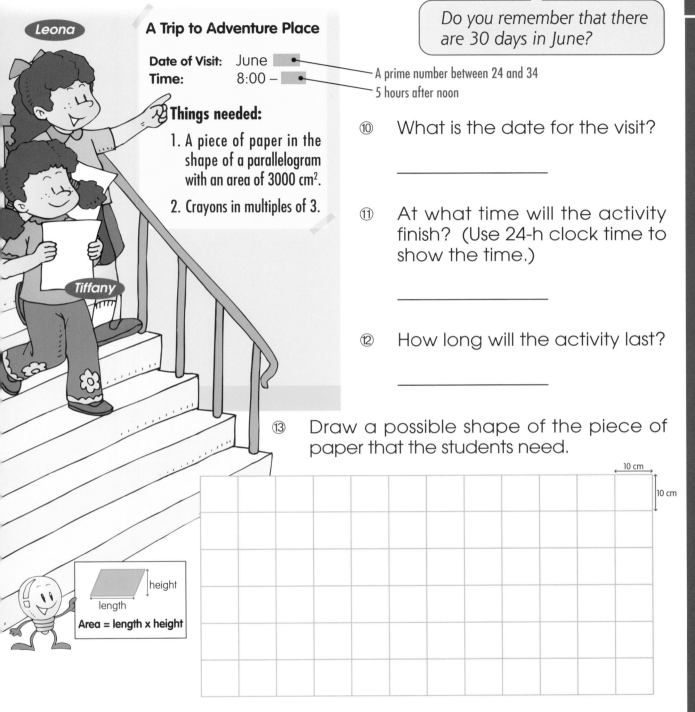

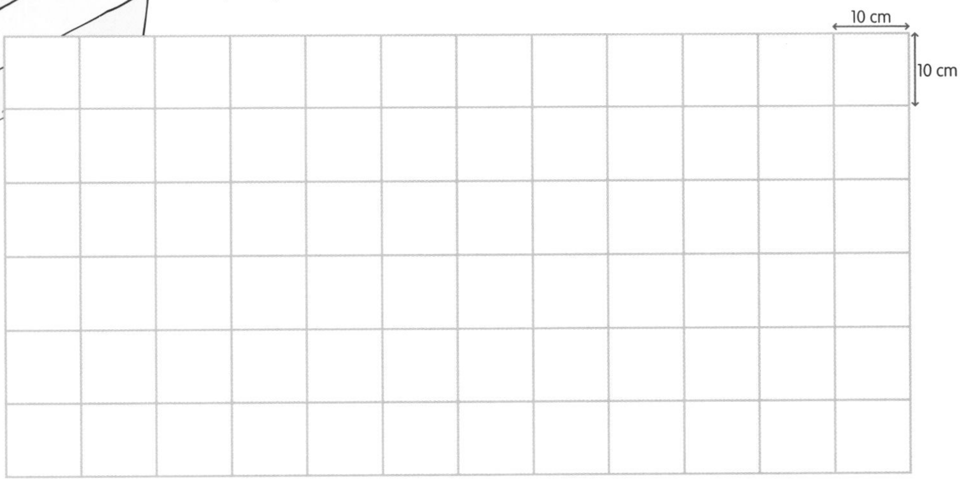

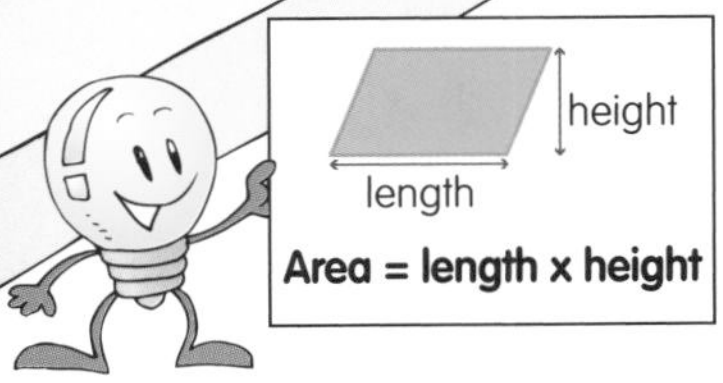

⑭ Which boxes of crayons should the students take with them? Check ✔ the correct letters.

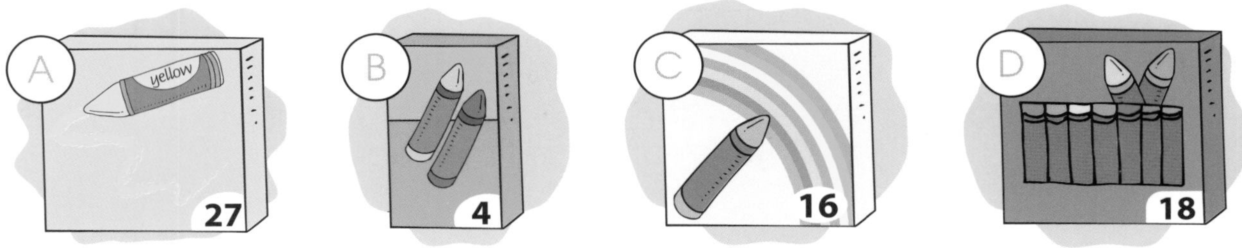

The children are going to Adventure Place today. Look at the map. Write the letters to show the places on the map. Then answer the questions.

⑮

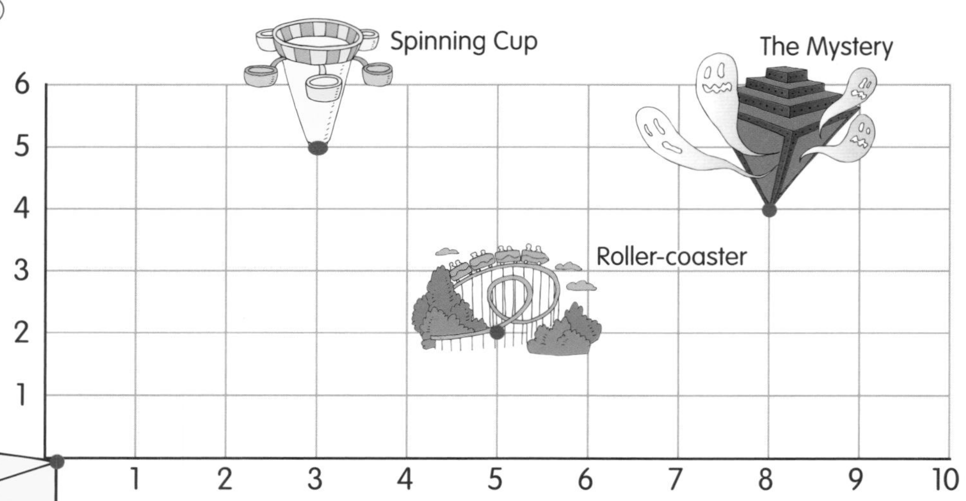

A Action Theatre **(0, 4)**

B Picnic Area **(9, 2)**

C Ferris Wheel **(2, 0)**

⑯ Write the coordinates.

a. The entrance ________ b. Spinning Cup ________

c. The Mystery ________ d. Roller-coaster ________

⑰ The Mystery and the Roller-coaster are about 400 m apart. The distance between the Ferris Wheel and the Roller-coaster is about ________ m or ________ km apart.

1 km = 1000 m; 0.1 km = 100 m

Action Theatre

Movie	Starts at
A	11:45
B	13:35
C	15:05

⑱ Movie A ends at 12:37. How long does it last?

____

⑲ Movie B lasts 23 minutes. What is the finishing time?

____

⑳ Joseph wants to watch Movie C. If he wants to be at Action Theatre 10 minutes before show time, at what time should he be there?

____

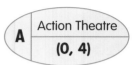

Mrs. Martin gives each group of students an assignment. Once the assignment is completed, the children can enjoy the rides. Help the children work out their assignments.

㉑ Ferris Wheel facts

- There are 12 cars on the wheel; 5 cars are blue and the rest are red. The ratio of blue cars to that of red ones is ______ .
- The wheel rotates at a rate of 4 revolutions/min. It rotates ______ revolutions in 4 minutes.

㉒ The Mystery facts

- The structure below is the model of the top part of The Mystery. Find the volume of each layer.

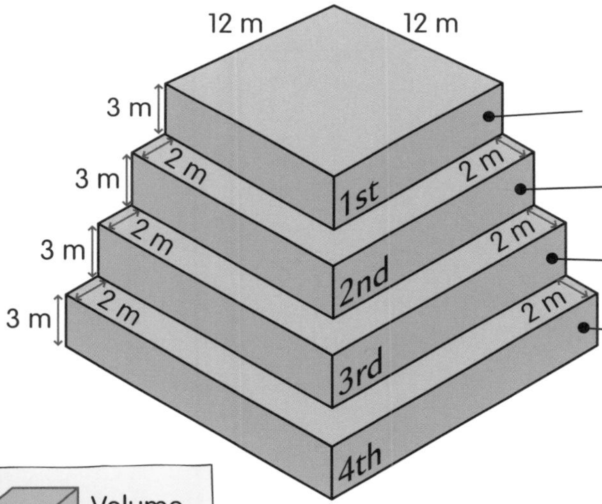

V: ______________

V: ______________

V: ______________

V: ______________

If the pattern continues, the volume of the 5th layer will be______________.

- The capacity of each layer is 10 people fewer than double that of the previous layer. If the capacity of the 1st layer is 25 people, the 2nd layer is ______________. The 3rd layer is ______________ and the 4th layer is ______________ .

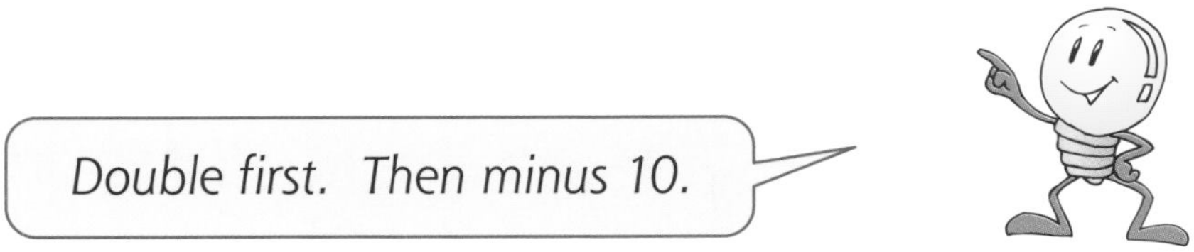

Look at the model of the Ferris Wheel. Help the children find the orders of rotational symmetry of the Ferris Wheel and the shapes. Then answer the questions.

㉓ The order of the rotational symmetry of the Ferris Wheel is __________ .

Rotational symmetry of order 3.
It fits on itself 3 times in one complete rotation.

㉔ Write in the circles the order of the rotational symmetry of the shapes the children made.

a.

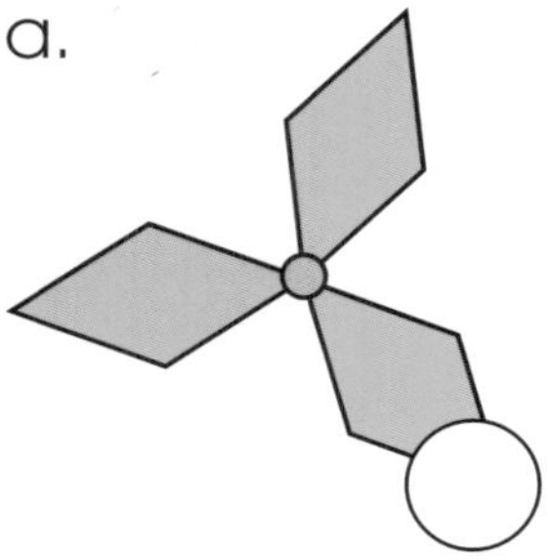

b.

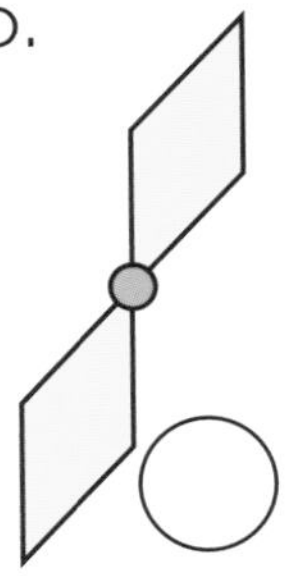

c.

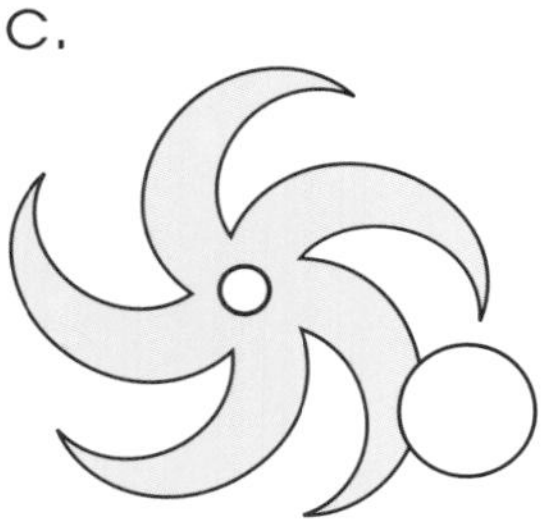

d.

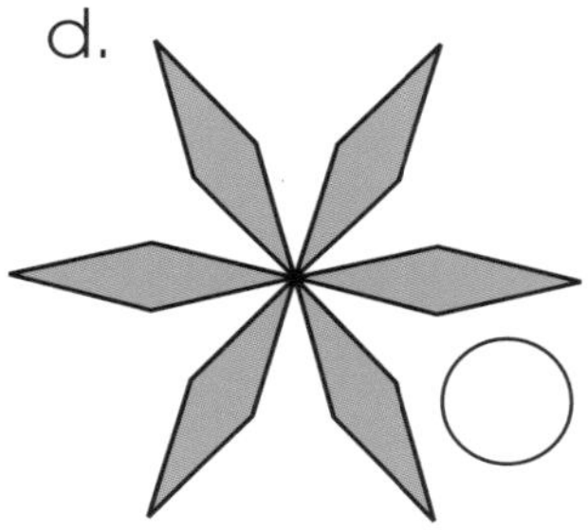

e.

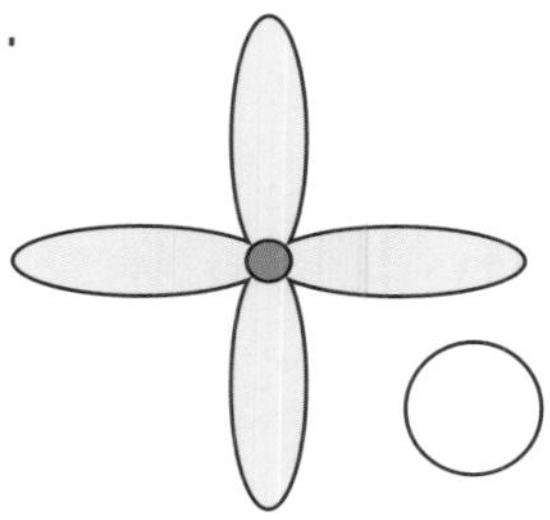

Help the children colour the shapes to complete their last activity.

㉕ Colour $\frac{1}{6}$ of the shape green and 50% yellow.

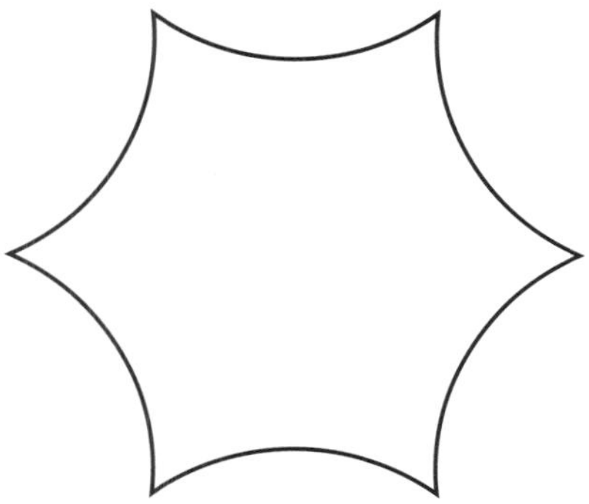

㉖ Colour 0.2 of the shape orange and 40% blue.

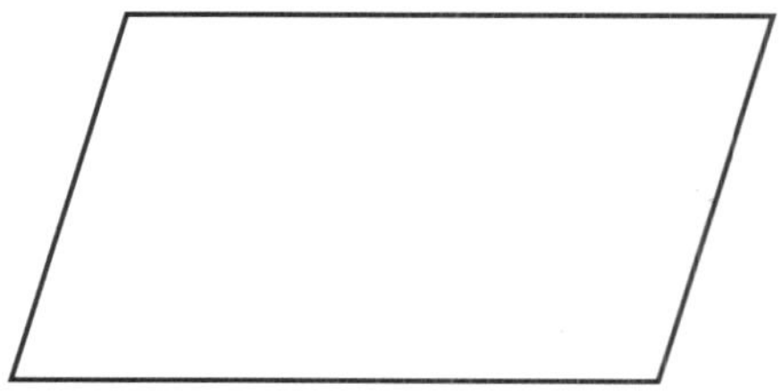

Help the children fill in the blanks.

㉗ The track length is 395 ______ (mm cm m km).

㉘ If the roller-coaster travels at its maximum speed for $\frac{1}{2}$ h, the total distance travelled will be ______ km.

㉙ There are 6 carts on a train. Each cart can carry 4 riders. The capacity of the train is ______ people.

㉚ If the train is full with 16 children and the rest are adults, the ratio of adults to children is ______ . (Write the ratio in simplest form.)

Find out how many adults are on the train first.

Leona and Jason are on the train now. Look at the pictures. Help them find out the duration of the ride. Then answer the questions.

㉛

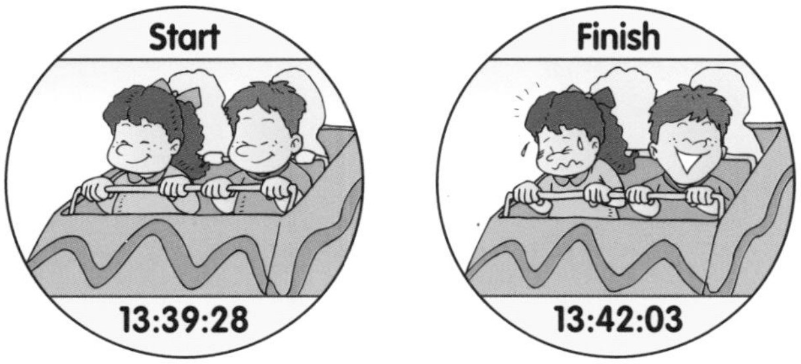

Duration: ______ min ______ s

㉜ 4 out of 20 or ______ % of the riders want to go on the ride again.

㉝ Number of riders on 6 rides:

24	19	24	23	21	15

Mean: ______ riders

Mode: ______ riders

Median: ______ riders

Find the children's favourite drinks. Then answer the questions.

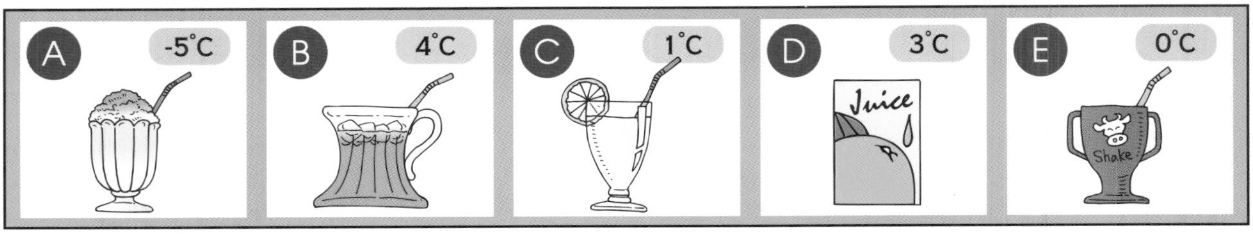

㉞ Leona is going to buy the coldest drink. She would like to have ______ . The temperature of this drink is ______ °C; it is ______ °C below / above 0°C.

㉟ Jason wants to have a drink with a temperature higher than 2°C. He can order either ______ or ______ .

Complete the tree diagram to show all the possible combinations of the Good Deal Combo. Then answer the questions.

㊱

Drink	*Snack*	*Combo*
A	*Popcorn*	*A + Popcorn*
	Fries	*A + Fries*
B		
C		
D		
E		

㊲ What is the probability of a customer choosing a combo with fries?

______

㊳ What is the probability of a customer choosing a combo with C ?

______

㊴ If Leona and Jason share the cost of a combo, how much does each person need to pay? (Correct to 2 decimal places.)

______

Today is 'Take Your Kid To Work Day'. Gary is at his father's office. Help Gary draw all the lines of symmetry for the shape on the picture. Then answer the questions.

①

② What is the order of rotational symmetry of the shape on the picture?

____

③ If the length of the frame is 30 cm and is 2 times the width, what is the area of the frame?

____

④ What is the estimated cost for renovating ABC Warehouse? (Write the amount in words.)

____

____

⑤ How many tonnes of cement will Gary's father order?

____

⑥ At what time should Gary's father give John a call?

____

⑦ Draw the model on the isometric dot paper.

Gary's father has a meeting with his client. Look at the model. Help Gary's father complete the net and answer the questions.

⑧ Complete the net to show the solid of the top part of the model.

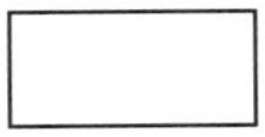

⑨ Complete each tiling by drawing the tiles on each grid.

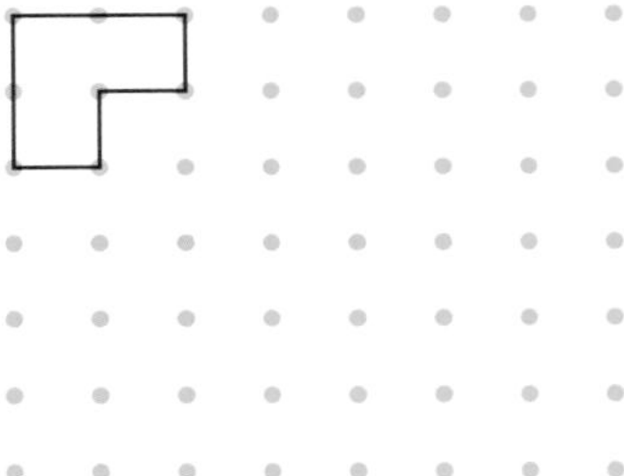

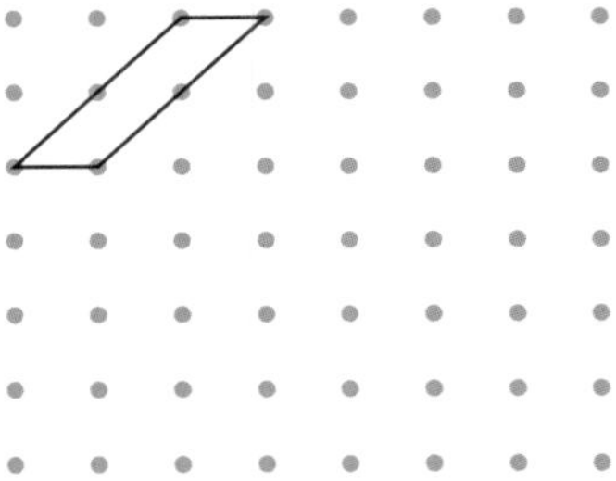

⑩ 465 tiles are needed to cover each floor. How many tiles are needed to cover 16 floors?

____________ tiles

Gary helps his father do the colouring to show the pattern on the wallpaper. Write each coloured part as a fraction, a decimal, and a percent.

⑪

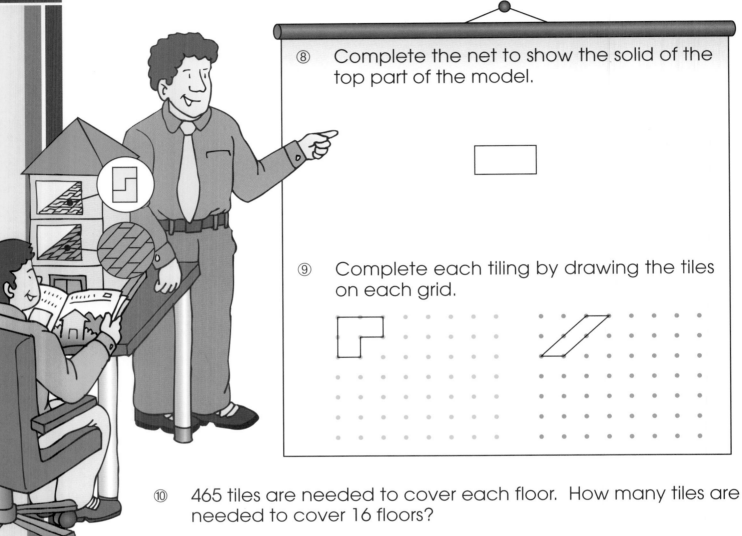

______ ______ ______

⑫

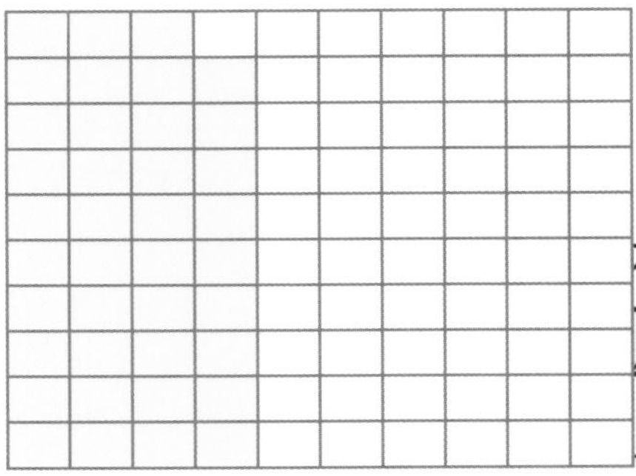

______ ______ ______

Gary helps his father make photocopies of his documents. Help Gary solve the problems.

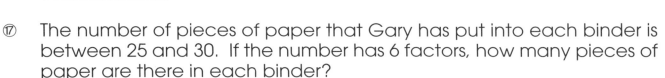

Initial reading: 9867
Final reading: 10329

⑬ How many copies has Gary made?

_____________ copies

⑭ If Gary takes 5 seconds to make 15 copies, what is his rate of making copies?

_____________ copies/second

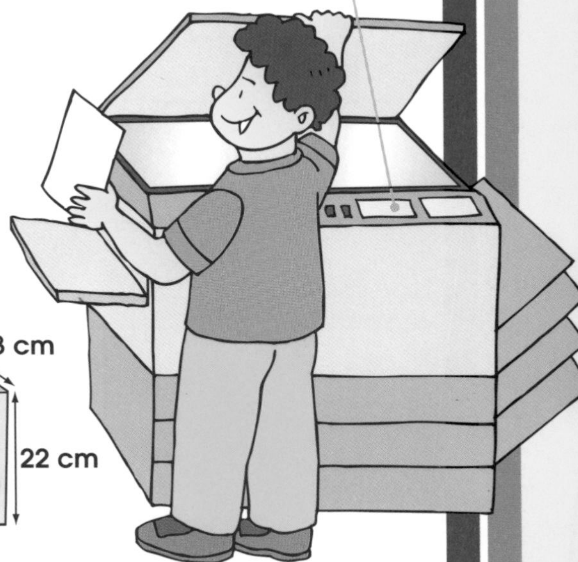

⑮ What is the volume of the box containing the paper?

_____________ cm^3

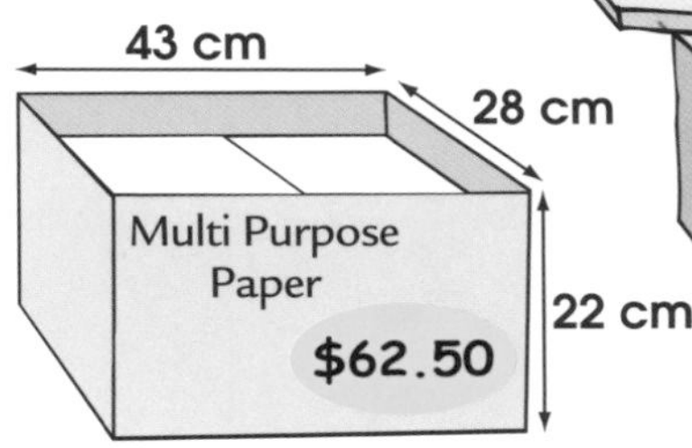

⑯ There are 10 packs of paper in the box. How much does each pack of paper cost?

$ _____________

⑰ The number of pieces of paper that Gary has put into each binder is between 25 and 30. If the number has 6 factors, how many pieces of paper are there in each binder?

_____________ pieces

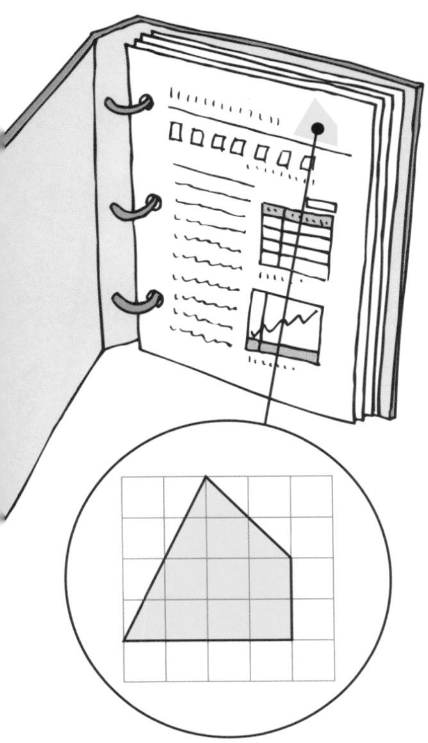

⑱ Draw one congruent and one similar figure for the logo on the letterhead.

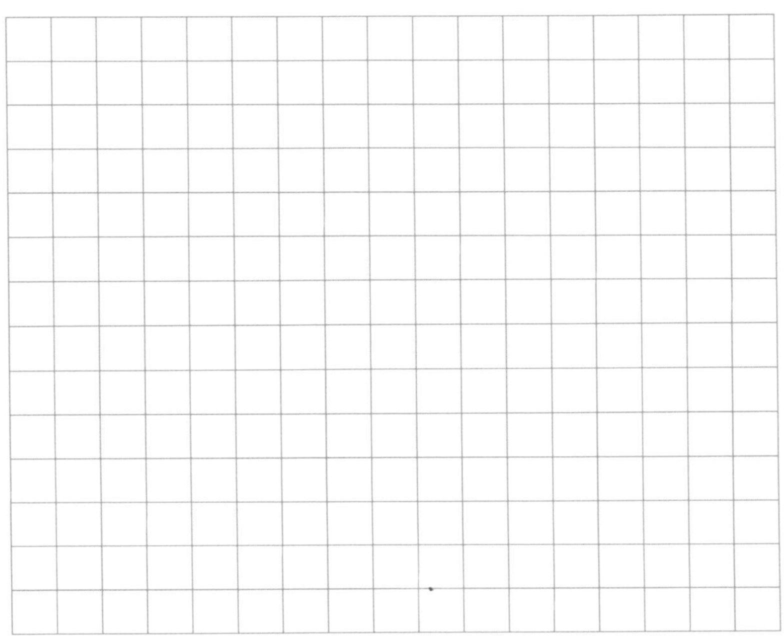

Gary is having lunch with his father in the kitchen. Look at the things in the kitchen. Help Gary solve the problems.

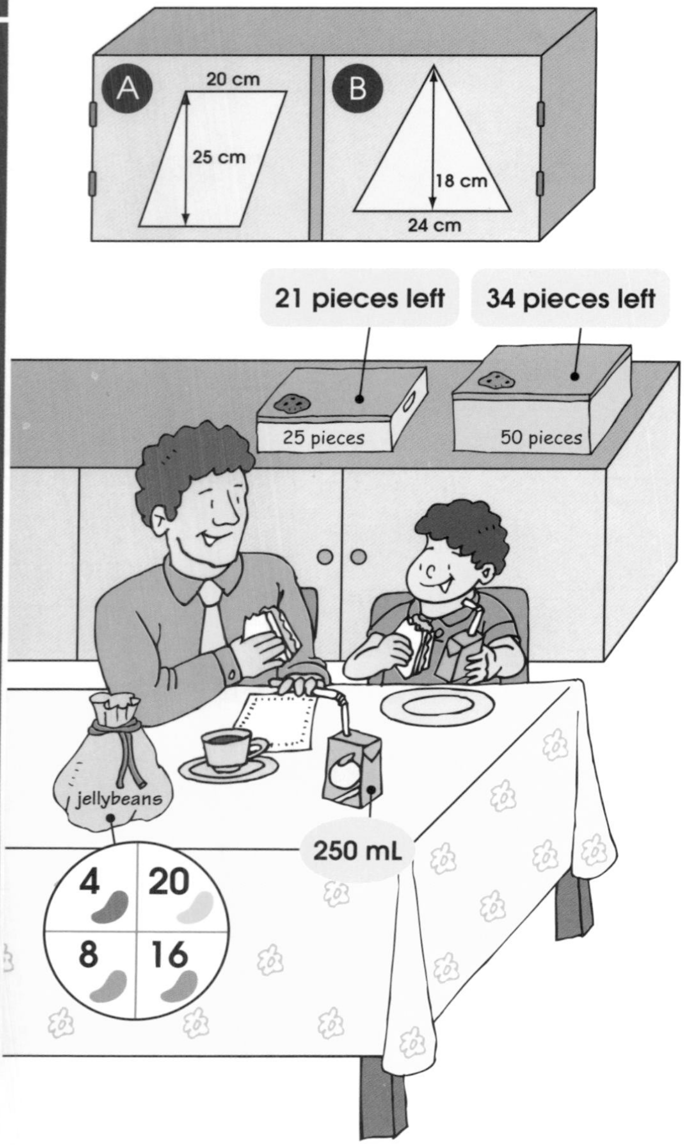

⑲ Find the areas of the shapes on the cupboard.

Ⓐ : ____________ cm^2

Ⓑ : ____________ cm^2

⑳ What percent of the cookies in the small box are left?

____

㉑ What percent of the cookies in the big box are eaten?

____

㉒ If Gary starts eating his sandwich at 13:05:16 and finishes it at 13:11:25, how long does he take to finish the sandwich?

____

㉓ There is 123.65 mL of juice in the box. How much juice has been drunk?

____

Colour the circle graph to show the number of jellybeans in each colour. Help Gary find the probability of picking jellybeans.

㉔ No. of Jellybeans in Each Colour

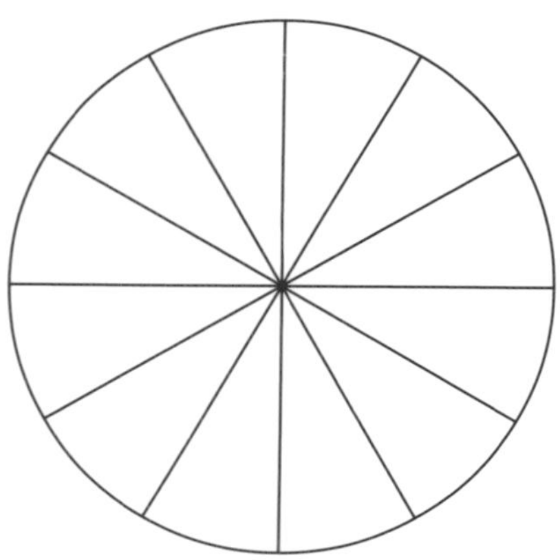

㉕ The probability of picking a jellybean in

a. red ______

b. purple or yellow ______

c. brown ______

d. a colour that is not green ______

Gary and his father are going to the construction site. Look at the map showing the buildings around his father. Help Gary solve the problems.

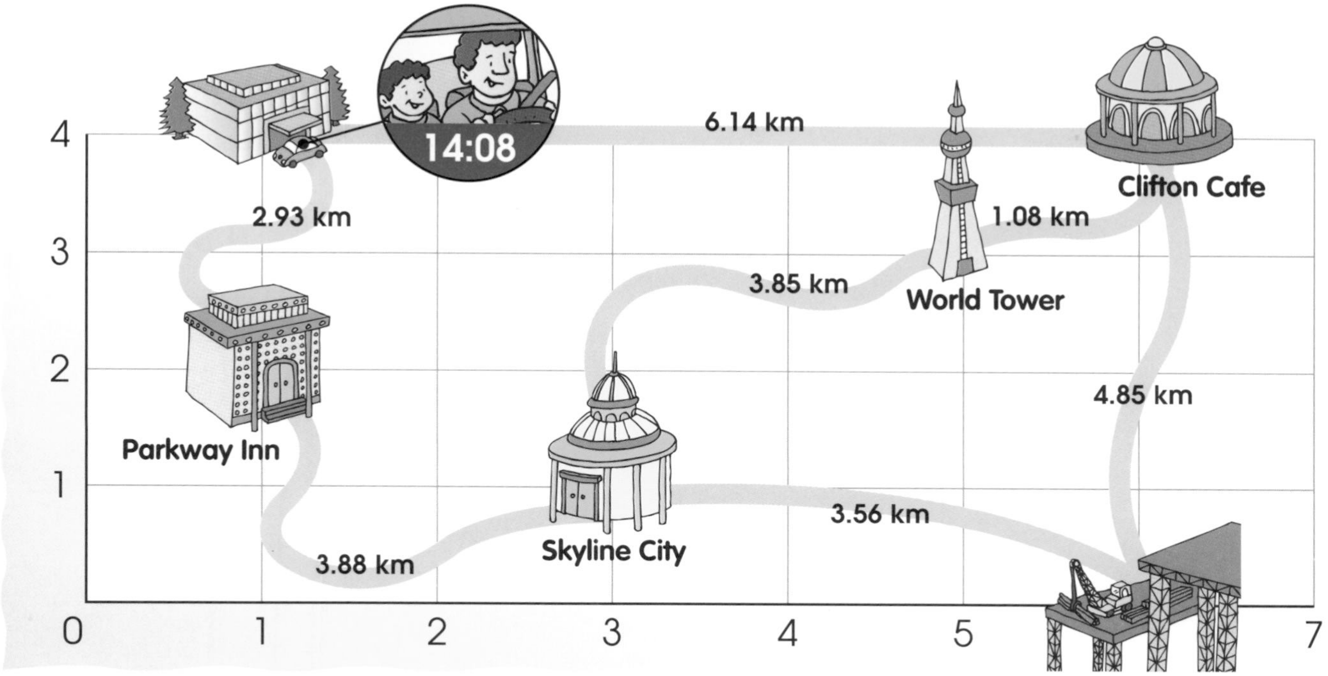

㉖ Gary's father drives from his office to the construction site by the shortest route. What is the distance travelled? Describe the places he passes by.

____

____

㉗ If Gary's father arrives at the construction site at 14:36, how long does he take to drive to the site?

____

㉘ A worker earns $107.10 for 6 hours of work. If he works 5 hours, how much does he earn?

____

㉙ A worker works $3\frac{7}{12}$ hours in the morning and $3\frac{3}{4}$ hours in the afternoon. How many hours does he work a day? (Write the answer in simplest form.)

____

Gary shows his father a report about his day when his father is working on a graph. Look at the graph and help Gary answer the questions.

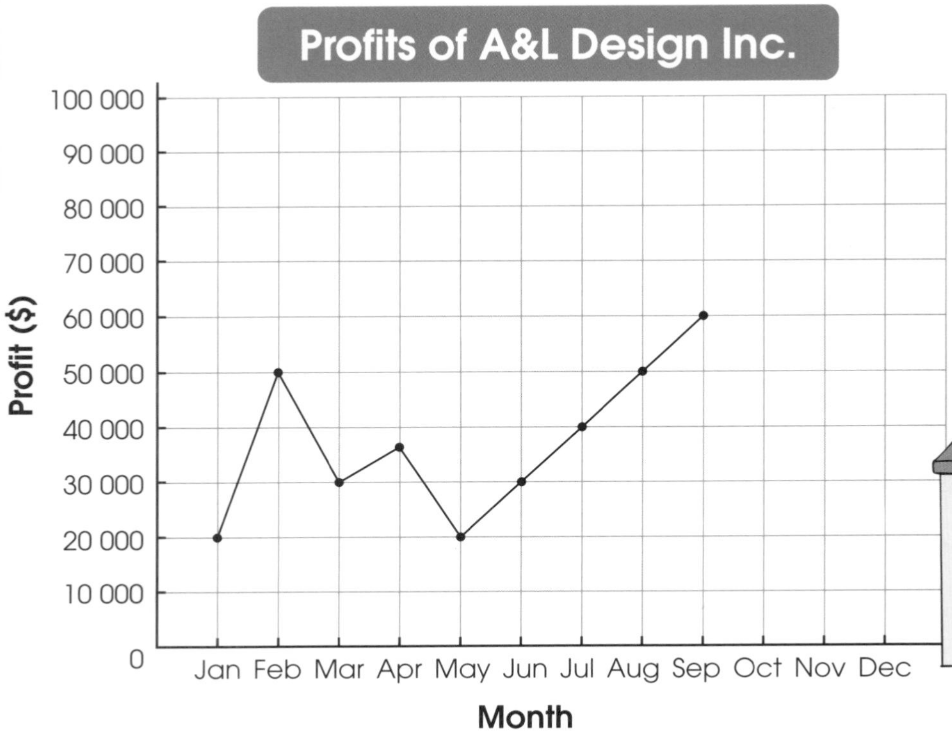

30. In multiples of what number is the vertical scale of the graph? __________

31. How many months are there in which the profit was over $45 000? __________

32. From January to September, what is the median profit? __________

33. If the profits made follow a pattern, what will the profit be in December? __________

34. What is the ratio of the profit made in May to the profit made in February? __________

35. How long did Gary take to write his report? __________

36. There are 350 words in Gary's report. What is his rate of writing? __________

1 Operations with Whole Numbers

1. ten thousands ; 30 000 ; 100 000 + 30 000 + 200 + 1
2. hundred thousands ; 600 000 ; 600 000 + 100 + 10 + 3
3. thousands ; 2000 ; 700 000 + 80 000 + 2000 + 3
4. < 5. < 6. <
7. > 8. > 9. <
10. 966 430 11. 554 739 12. 604 762
13. 780 653 14. 849 15. 1249
16. 3763 17. 34 109 18. 39 062
19. 36 233 20. 4884 21. 14 811
22. 5099
23. 4005 ; 1000 + 1000 + 1000 + 1000 = 4000
24. 7640 ; 3000 + 1000 + 1000 + 3000 = 8000
25. 29 260 ; 38 000 – 8000 = 30 000
26. ; 1596

```
   133
 x  12
   266
  1330
  1596
```

27.

```
   124
 x  39
  1116
  3720
  4836
```

28.

```
   768
 x  25
  3840
 15360
 19200
```

29.

```
   981
 x  47
  6867
 39240
 46107
```

30. 20 570 31. 45 408
32. 19 293 33. 6552
34. 11 853 ; 440 x 30 = 13 200
35. 40 092 ; 770 x 50 = 38 500
36. 27 765 ; 620 x 50 = 31 000
37. 134 ; 134 ;

```
      134
12)1608
   12
    40
    36
     48
     48
```

38.

```
     102
46)4692
   46
     92
     92
```

39.

```
      41
39)1599
   156
     39
     39
```

40.

```
     338R17
25)8467
   75
    96
    75
    217
    200
     17
```

41.

```
     164R1
18)2953
   18
   115
   108
     73
     72
      1
```

42.

```
     291R7
23)6700
   46
   210
   207
     30
     23
      7
```

43. 189 44. 236R14
45. 137R20 46. 96
47. 122R8 ; 36 x 125 = 4500
48. ✔ ; 24 x 216 = 5184
49. 1080 ÷ 60 = 18 ; 18
50. 452 + 386 + 415 + 339 = 1592 ; 1592
51. 678 x 11 = 7458 ; 7458
52. 1592 – 678 = 914 ; 914
53. 914 x 25 = 22 850 ; 22 850
54. 22 850 – 7458 = 15 392 ; 15 392
55. 14 ; 42 ; 56 56. 12 ; 11 ; 1
57. 83 ; 8 ; 75 58. 69 + 10 ; 79
59. 91 – 68 ; 23 60. 90 – 3 x 28 = 6 ; 6
61. 4 x 3 + 19 = 31 ; 31

Activity

9

2 Brackets

1. 4 ; 7 ; 18 ; 18 2. 20 ; 35 ; 175 ; 175
3. 17 – 4 ; 13 4. 4 x 7 ; 28
5. 48 ÷ 3 ; 16 6. 14 + 14 ; 28
7. 76 ÷ 2 ; 38 8. 20 x 8 ; 160
9. 99 + (33 ÷ 11) = 102 10. (108 – 3) x 9 = 945
11. 14 x (7 + 6) = 182 12. 256 ÷ (16 – 8) = 32
13. 100 – (36 ÷ 4) = 91 14. 39 + (2 x 17) = 73
15. 3 ; 5 ; 21 ; 35 ; 56
16. 18 ; 7 ; 72 ; 28 ; 44
17. 31 ; 15 ; 279 ; 135 ; 144
18. 50 ; 2 ; 250 ; 10 ; 260

Activity

1. 546 2. 531 ; 59 = 60 – 1
3. 544 ; 68 = 70 – 2 4. 294 ; 42 = 40 + 2
5. 415 ; 83 = 80 + 3

3 Integers

1. 12, -3, 0, 8, 156, -8, 20
2. -6 3. +15 4. +36
5. -14 6. +9 7. -87
8. > 9. < 10. <
11. > 12. > 13. <
14. -6, -3, 0, 2, 5
15. -4, 1, 3, 5, 7
16. -5, -3, 0, 1, 6
17. A : -2°C B : 3°C C : 9°C
D : 1°C E : -3°C F : 4°C
18. C 19. 2
20. 4 21. C
22. E, A, D, B, F, C

Activity

1. -1 ; 5 2. 0 ; -4
3. -6 ; -9

4 Multiples and Factors

1. 6 ; 8 ; 10 ; 12 ; 14 ; 16
2. 9 ; 12 ; 15
3. 5, 10, 15, 20, 25, 30
4. 7, 14, 21, 28, 35, 42
5. 9, 18, 27, 36, 45, 54

6a. 4 : 4, 8, 12, 16, 20, 24, 28, 32
6 : 6, 12, 18, 24, 30, 36, 42, 48

b. 12, 24 c. 12

7a. 8 : 8, 16, 24, 32, 40, 48, 56, 64
10 : 10, 20, 30, 40, 50, 60, 70, 80
b. 40 c. 40
8. 20, 40, 60, 80 ; 20
9. 9, 18, 27, 36 ; 9
10. 6, 12, 18, 24 ; 6
11. 14 12. 7
13. 2 14. 1
15. 1, 2, 7, 14
16. 12 ; 6 ; 4 ; 1, 2, 3, 4, 6, 12
17. 20 ; 10 ; 5 ; 1, 2, 4, 5, 10, 20
18. 1, 2, 3, 4, 6, 8, 12, 24
19. 1, 2, 3, 5, 6, 10, 15, 30
20. 1, 2, 4, 8, 16, 32
21. 1, 2, 3, 4, 6, 9, 12, 18, 36
22. 1, 2, 4, 5, 8, 10, 20, 40
23a. 20 : 1, 2, 4, 5, 10, 20
28 : 1, 2, 4, 7, 14, 28
b. 1, 2, 4 c. 4
24a. 25 : 1, 5, 25
45 : 1, 3, 5, 9, 15, 45
b. 1, 5 c. 5
25. 1, 5 ; 5 26. 1, 2, 4, 8 ; 8

Activity

6 ; 4 ; 5

5 *Composite and Prime Numbers*

1. 7 ; prime 2. 5 ; prime
3. 4 ; composite 4. composite
5. prime 6. composite
7. prime 8. composite
9. composite

10.
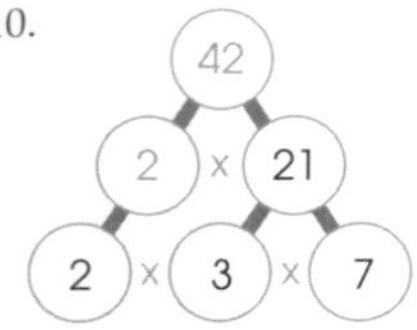

; 2 x 3 x 7

11.
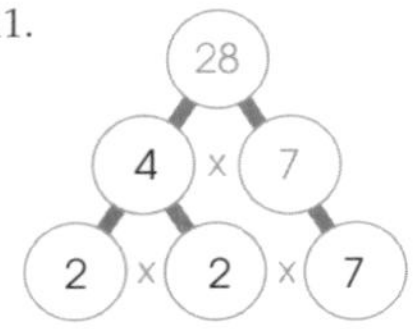

; 2 x 2 x 7

12.
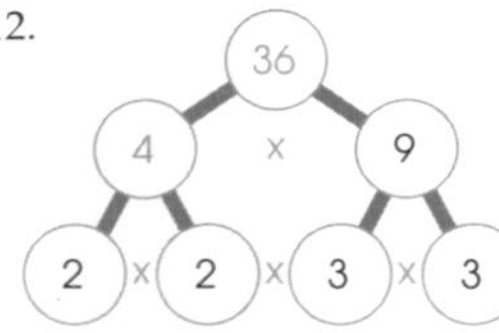

; 2 x 2 x 3 x 3

13.
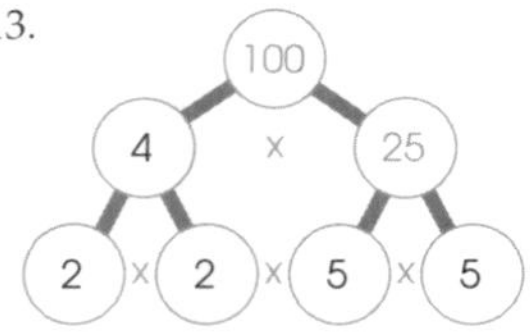

; 2 x 2 x 5 x 5

14. 2 x 3 x 11 15. 2 x 2 x 13
16. 2 x 37 17. 2 x 2 x 2 x 2 x 2 x 3
18. 3 x 3 x 3 x 3 19. 2 x 2 x 2 x 11
20. 2 x 2 x 2 x 2 x 2 21. 2 x 2 x 2 x 5
22. 2 x 2 x 2 x 3 23. 2 x 29
24. 2, 3, 5 ;
3, 3, 5 ;
3, 5 ;
3, 5 ; 15
25. 2, 2, 2, 2, 3 ;
2, 2, 2, 3, 3 ;
2, 2, 2, 3 ;
2, 2, 2, 3 ; 24
26. 2 x 2 x 3 ; 2 x 2 x 5 ; 4
27. 3 x 5 ; 2 x 2 x 3 x 5 ; 15
28. 2 x 2 x 2 ; 2 x 2 x 2 x 5 ; 8
29. 2 x 2 x 2 x 7 ; 2 x 2 x 2 x 2 x 2 x 2 ; 8
30. 2, 5 ;
2, 3, 11 ;
2, 3, 5, 11 ;
330
31. 5 ;
2, 5, 5 ;
2, 5, 5, 7 ;
350
32. 3, 5 ;
3, 7 ;
3, 5, 7 ;
105
33. 30 34. 40
35. 72 36. 54
37. 66 38. 216

Activity

1-3. (Suggested answers)
1. 5, 19 2. 29, 47
3. 31, 59

6 *Time, Speed, and Distance*

1. A : 13:30 B : 12:15
C : 16:45 D : 03:18
E : 19:53 F : 21:27

2.

; 2:20:10 p.m.

3.

; 12:47:13 a.m.

4. No 5. 40 min
6. 12:15 7. 16:39
8. 68 min or 1 h 8 min
9. CP826 10. 38 min
11. (Suggested answer)
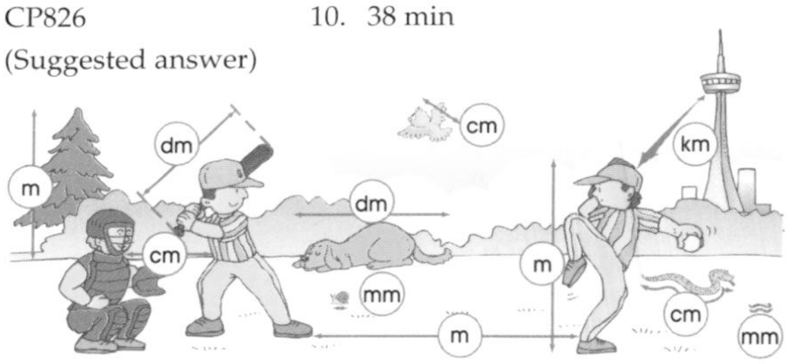

12. 630 13. 4000
14. 92 15. 57
16. 9.7 17. 2.3
18. 5.5 19. 3.71
20. 0.105 21. 80
22. 1270 23. 635
24. 1905
25.

Race	Distance	Time	Speed
1	700 km	2 h	$\frac{700}{2}$ = 350 (km/h)
2	347 000 m	1 h	$\frac{347}{1}$ = 347 (km/h)
3	414 km	1.2 h	345 km/h
4	531 km	1.5 h	354 km/h

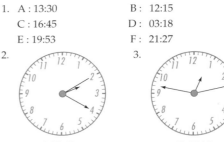

26. Race 4
27. 5 more km
28. 414 km/h
29. 540 s
30. 12:07 p.m.

Activity

43.6 m

7 *Perimeter and Area*

1. A : 5 cm ; 3 cm ; 15 cm^2
   B : 2 cm ; 2 cm ; 4 cm^2
   C : 3 cm ; 4 cm ; 12 cm^2
   D : 6 cm ; 3 cm ; 9 cm^2
   E : 5 cm ; 4 cm ; 10 cm^2
   F : 4 cm ; 2 cm ; 4 cm^2
2. Yes
3. Yes
4. A : 5 cm ; 6 cm ; 30 cm^2 ; 24 cm
   B : 7 cm ; 12 cm ; 84 cm^2 ; 40 cm
   C : 28 cm ; 38 cm ; 1064 cm^2 ; 142 cm
   D : 12 m ; 9 m ; 108 m^2 ; 44 m
   E : 18 km ; 3 km ; 54 km^2 ; 43 km
5. (Suggested answer)

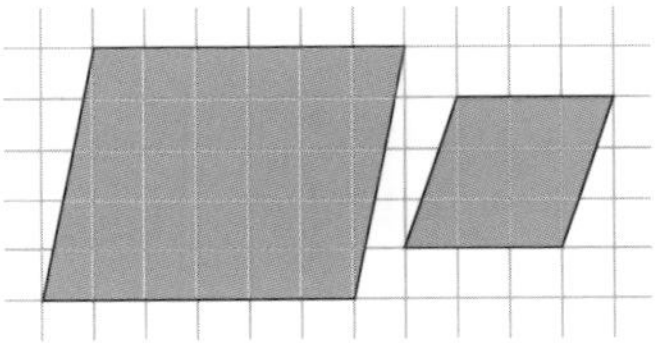

6. A : 4.6 cm ; 7.5 cm ; 17.25 cm^2 ; 20.9 cm
   B : 12 cm ; 7 cm ; 42 cm^2 ; 31 cm
   C : 5 cm ; 5 cm ; 12.5 cm^2 ; 20.7 cm
   D : 3 m ; 4 m ; 6 m^2 ; 13.9 m
7. D, B, A, C
8. B, C, A, D
9. (Suggested answer)

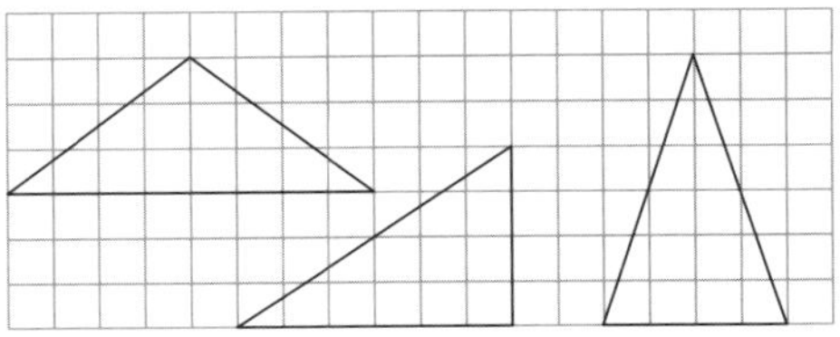

10. 13
11. 64
12. 500

Activity

32

8 *2-D Shapes and 3-D Figures*

1.

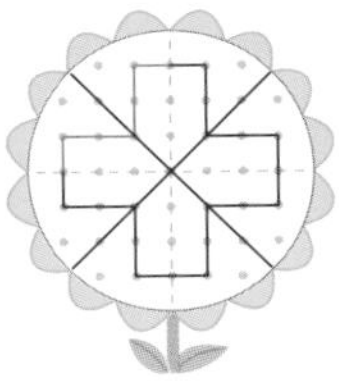

2.

3. (Suggested answers)

a.

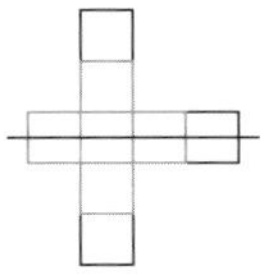

b.

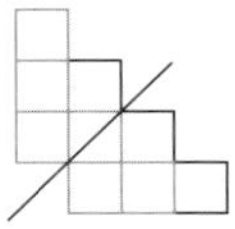

c.

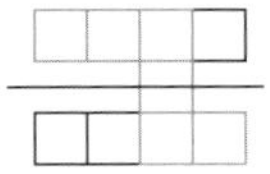

4. 2 ; 5 ; 2
   3 ; 4 ; 4
5. (Suggested answer)

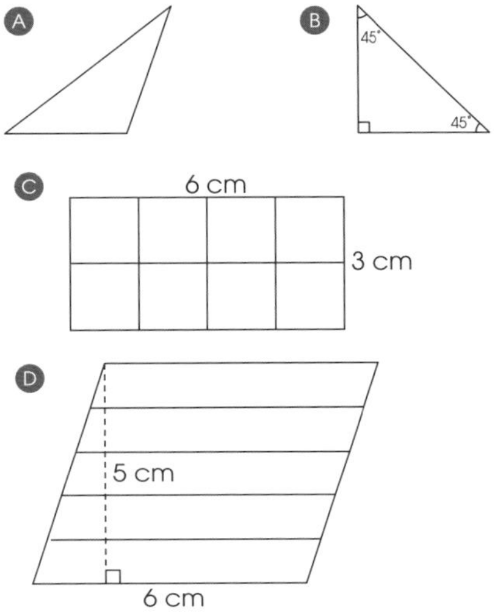

6-7. (Draw shapes with the same sizes and shapes as the given ones.)
8. 1 ; 4 ; 2 ; 6
9. (Suggested answers)

10. A, C
11. C
12. A, C
13.

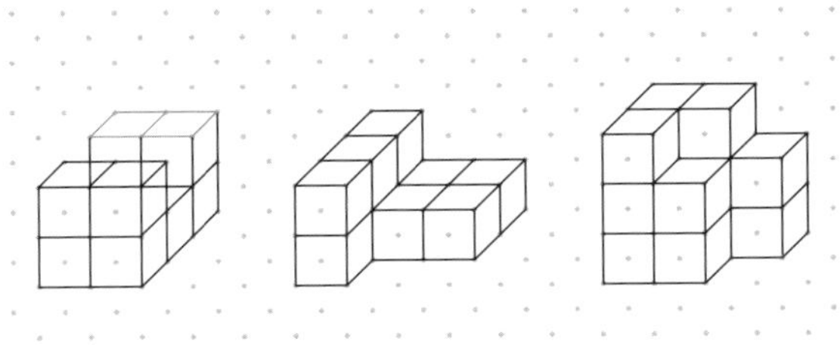

Activity

Yes, since they are different sizes. But the corresponding angles of the triangles are the same.

Midway Test

1. 8 ; 7 ; 72 ; 63 ; 135
2. 3 ; 3 ; 348 ; 87 ; 261
3. 34 ÷ 17 ;
   = 2
4. 18 + 80 ;
   = 98
5. 110 – 60 ;
   = 50
6. 50 ÷ 2 ;
   = 25
7. 7 : 7, 14, 21, 28, 35, 42, 49, 56
   8 : 8, 16, 24, 32, 40, 48, 56, 64
   56 ; 56
8. 6 : 6, 12, 18, 24, 30, 36, 42, 48
   9 : 9, 18, 27, 36, 45, 54, 63, 72
   18, 36 ; 18
9.
```
      366
 25)9150
    75
    165
    150
     150
     150
```
10.
```
      76R21
 37)2833
    259
     243
     222
      21
```
11.
```
    782
 x   32
   1564
  23460
  25024
```
12. 32 665
13. 421R2
14. 4727
15. 222R1
16. 90 km/h
17. 225 km
18. 18:05
19. 20 : 1, 2, 4, 5, 10, 20
    32 : 1, 2, 4, 8, 16, 32
    1, 2, 4 ;
    4
20. 18 : 1, 2, 3, 6, 9, 18
    24 : 1, 2, 3, 4, 6, 8, 12, 24
    1, 2, 3, 6 ;
    6
21. -3°C
22. No
23. Tomorrow

24-25. (Suggested answers)

24.
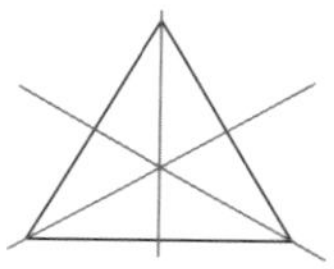

25.
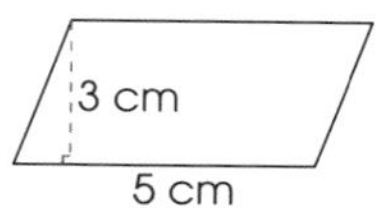

26a.
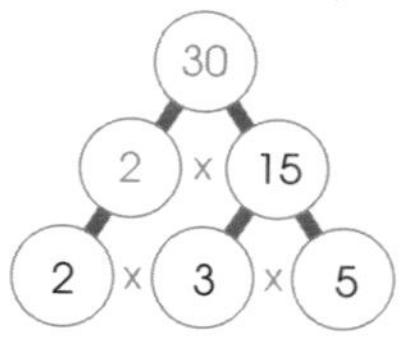

; 2 x 3 x 5

b.
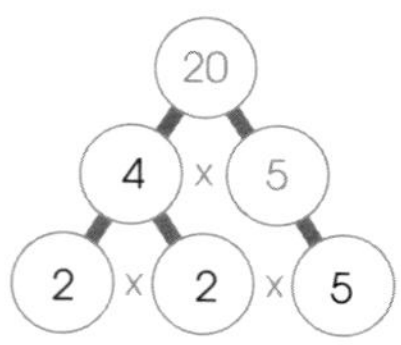

; 2 x 2 x 5

c.
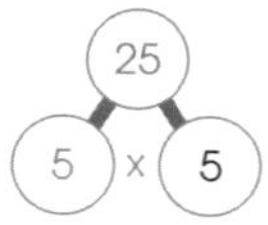

; 5 x 5

27. 10
28. 5
29. 60
30. 100
31. 6
32. 3
33. 35 069
34. 900
35. 87 848
36. 2465
37. 80 cm^2 ; 44 cm
38. 48 m^2 ; 32 m
39. (Suggested answer)

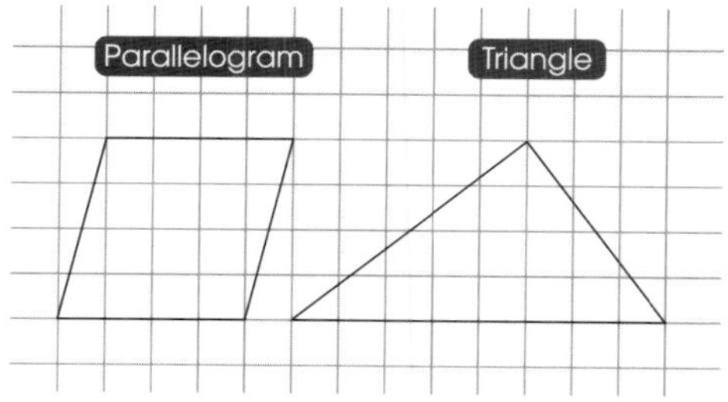

40.
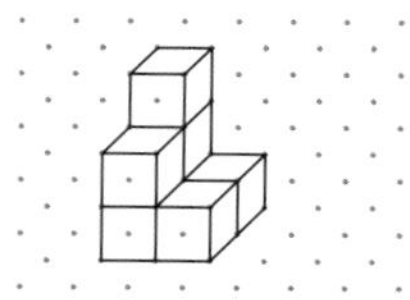

41.
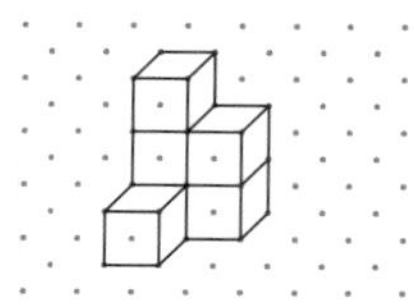

42.
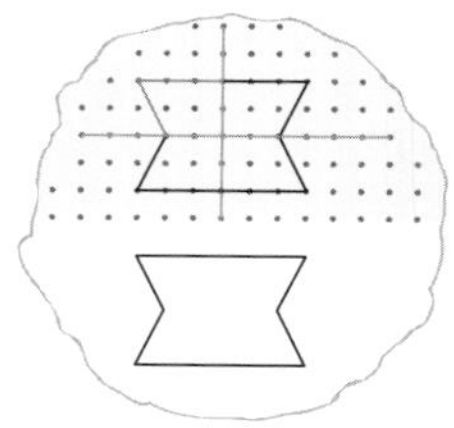

43.
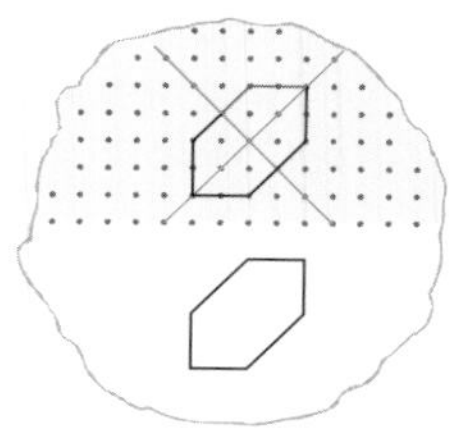

44. 13 x 927 = 12 051 ; He will make $12 051.
45. 13 000 – 4662 = 8338 ; He will earn $8338.
46. 3348 ÷ 31 = 108 ; 108 pizzas are sold in a day.

9 *Volume and Mass*

1. A : 36 m^3 B : 768 cm^3
   C : 255 cm^3 D : 420 cm^3
   E : 297 cm^3
2. 324
3. 1750 ; 440
4. 9008
5. 4.39
6. 6145
7. 0.978
8. 17 240
9. 0.9
10. 1260
11. 2
12. George: 7500 g
    Louis: 8 kg
    Wayne: 995 mg
    Richard: 5.1 kg
    Bob: 5.2 g
    Ted: 4975 mg
13. Louis
14. Wayne

Activity

295.2

10 *Operations with Decimals*

1. 40 + 5 + 0.6 + 0.01 + 0.009 ; 45 and 619 thousandths
2. 60 + 0.2 + 0.002 ; 60 and 202 thousandths
3. 4.251
4. 4.031
5. 0.167
6. 12.029
7. 2.585
8. 0.609
9. 8.934
10. 4.247
11. 4.771
12. 262.3
13. 0.388
14. 0.894
15. 76.7
16. 50.51
17. 3.054
18. 0.0625
19. 0.001
20. 2 ; 4 ; 7 ; 0 ; 2.47
21. 2.52
22. 2.600

23. 14.004
24. 11.286
25. 9.31
26. 26.145
27. 32.334
28. 11.284
29. 18.615
30. 3.6
31. 6.02
32. 1.92
33. 75 ; 5 ; 5

$$\begin{array}{r} 5 \\ 15\overline{)75} \\ \underline{75} \end{array}$$

34. $= \frac{32.4 \times 10}{0.4 \times 10} = \frac{324}{4} = 81$

$$\begin{array}{r} 81 \\ 4\overline{)324} \\ \underline{32} \\ 4 \\ \underline{4} \end{array}$$

35. $= \frac{1.6 \times 100}{0.08 \times 100} = \frac{160}{8} = 20$

$$\begin{array}{r} 20 \\ 8\overline{)160} \\ \underline{160} \end{array}$$

36. 177
37. 15
38. 0.17
39. 15.5
40. 6.2
41. 14
42. 18
43. 9
44. 4.02
45. 20.8
46. 4.414
47. 5.224
48. 13.3
49. 4.752
50. 26.7
51. 78.72
52. 7.423
53. 75.099
54. 64.4
55. 1.044

Activity

1. 2
2. 12.14
3. 5.3
4. 8.86
5. 3.4
6. 0

11 Operations with Fractions

1. $3\frac{2}{3}$
2. $\frac{31}{7}$
3. $\frac{9}{5}$
4. $\frac{13}{5}$
5. $1\frac{4}{9}$
6. $3\frac{1}{6}$
7. $\frac{7}{4}$
8. $2\frac{4}{7}$
9. $\frac{25}{8}$
10. $\frac{13}{2}$
11. $\frac{5}{2}$
12. $2\frac{7}{9}$
13. >
14. <
15. <
16. >
17. <
18. <
19. >
20. >
21. 3 ; 1
22. 4 ; 2
23. $\frac{6}{12}$; $\frac{1}{2}$
24. $\frac{7}{7}$; 1
25. $\frac{10}{15}$; $\frac{2}{3}$
26. $\frac{8}{20}$; $\frac{2}{5}$
27. $\frac{12}{10}$; $1\frac{1}{5}$
28. $\frac{16}{18}$; $\frac{8}{9}$
29. $1\frac{1}{3}$
30. $\frac{1}{4}$
31. $\frac{3}{5}$
32. $\frac{3}{8}$; $\frac{1}{4}$; $\frac{5}{8}$
33. $\frac{5}{6}$; $\frac{2}{3}$; $\frac{1}{6}$
34. $\frac{1}{2}$; $\frac{1}{3}$; $\frac{5}{6}$
35. $\frac{5}{6}$; $\frac{1}{3}$; $\frac{1}{2}$
36. 4 ; 5 ; $\frac{1}{2}$
37. 8 ; 5
38. $\frac{5}{8}$
39. $\frac{13}{20}$
40. $\frac{5}{6}$
41. $\frac{4}{15}$
42. $\frac{2}{5}$
43. $\frac{13}{15}$
44. $\frac{3}{16}$
45. $\frac{4}{5}$
46. $\frac{9}{16}$
47. $\frac{1}{8}$
48. $\frac{5}{6} + \frac{1}{3} = 1\frac{1}{6}$; $1\frac{1}{6}$
49. $\frac{17}{20} - \frac{3}{4} = \frac{1}{10}$; $\frac{1}{10}$
50. $\frac{9}{10} + \frac{1}{5} = 1\frac{1}{10}$; $1\frac{1}{10}$

Activity

No. of Days	1	2	3	4	5	6	7
Amount of Juice Consumed (L)	$\frac{2}{5}$	$\frac{4}{5}$	$\frac{6}{5}$	$\frac{8}{5}$	$\frac{10}{5}$	$\frac{12}{5}$	$\frac{14}{5}$

; 7

12 Fractions, Decimals, and Percents

1. 25%
2. 50%
3. 41%
4. 7%
5. 80%
6. 2%
7. 30%
8. 92%
9. 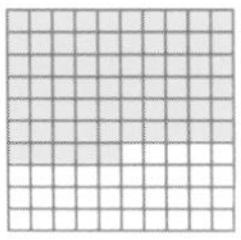
10. 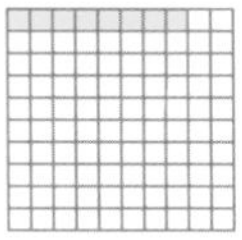
11. 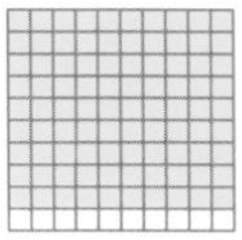
12. $\frac{71}{100}$; 0.71 ; 71%
13. $\frac{26}{100}$; 0.26 ; 26%
14. 13%
15. 57%
16. 8%
17. 35 ; 35%
18. 75 ; 75%
19. 32 ; 332%
20. 50 ; 450%
21. $1\frac{90}{100}$; 190%
22. $\frac{22}{100}$; 22%
23. $2\frac{25}{100}$; 225%
24. $1\frac{85}{100}$; 185%
25. $\frac{19}{50}$
26. $\frac{3}{5}$
27. $\frac{2}{25}$
28. $\frac{2}{5}$
29. $1\frac{9}{10}$
30. $2\frac{1}{2}$
31. 55 ; $\frac{11}{20}$
32. 25 ; $\frac{1}{4}$
33. 20 ; $\frac{1}{5}$

34a. 25
b. 20
c. 55

35. 20 ; 0.2
36. 5 ; 0.05
37. $\frac{77}{100}$; 0.77
38. $\frac{60}{100}$; 0.6
39. $\frac{125}{100}$; 1.25
40. $\frac{190}{100}$; 1.9
41. $\frac{142}{100}$; 1.42
42. $\frac{106}{100}$; 1.06
43. 34
44. 6
45. 80
46. 143
47. 120
48. 27
49. 604
50. 92
51. <
52. >
53. >
54. <
55. >
56. >
57. 40%, 0.55, $\frac{3}{5}$
58. 115%, 1.29, $1\frac{7}{20}$
59. 1.8%, $\frac{4}{25}$, 0.18
60. $\frac{2}{5}$; 40%
61. 50% ; 0.5
62. $\frac{1}{10}$; 0.1
63. 4%
64. 90%

Activity

1. Christmas

2a. 30%
b. 50%
c. 20%

13 Rate and Ratio

1. Pears: \$1.96/kg
   Grapes: \$3.28/kg
   Watermelons: \$0.87/kg
   Apples: \$1.74/kg
   Bananas: \$1.07/kg
   Oranges: \$2.62/kg
2. 4 for \$1.12
3. 3 for \$1.56
4. 5 for \$4.40
5. 3 ; 7
6. 2:7
7. 2:3
8. 3:12
9. 2:12
10. 7:12

11-16. (Suggested answers)

11. 4:6, 6:9
12. 10:8, 15:12
13. 1:3, 3:9
14. 4:3, 16:12
15. 4:3, 56:42
16. 2:5, 8:20
17. 1:2
18. 3:8
19. 4:7
20. 3:2
21. 3:5
22. 3:4
23. 8:1
24. 9:4

25a. 5:6
b. 2:3
c. 2:5
d. 4:15
e. 1:3

26a. 4:5
b. 10:9
c. 8:9
d. 3:1
e. 1:2
f. 2:3
g. 1:3
h. 1:3
i. 10:27

27. 1:1
28. 1:2
29. 1:1
30. 1:4
31. $0.56
32. $0.49
33. $6.45/kg

Activity

1. 1:3
2. 10
3. 3:1

14 *Patterns and Simple Equations*

1. 10 ; 31 ; 94 ; 283 ; 850
2. 20 ; 36 ; 68 ; 132 ; 260
3. 123 ; 366 ; 1095 ;
   Subtract 1 from the previous term and then multiply by 3
4. 287 ; 575 ; 1151 ;
   Multiply the previous term by 2 and then plus 1
5. 36 ; 28 ; 24 ;
   Divide the previous term by 2 and then plus 10
6. 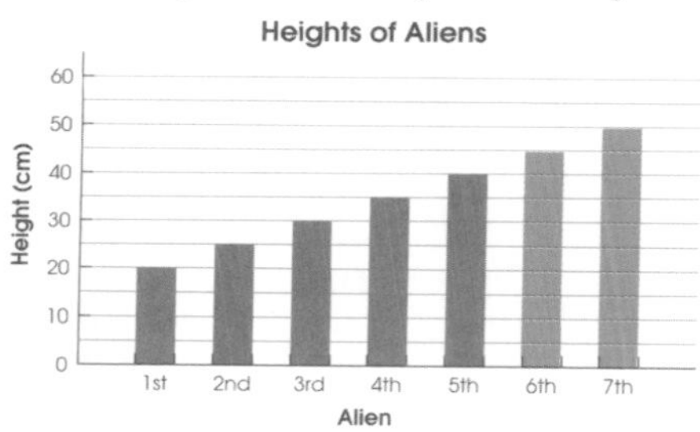

7. 50 cm
8. The 4th
9. The 5th
10. 60 cm
11. Each alien is 5 cm taller than the previous one.
12. 23 ; 28 ; 33 ; 38 ; 43 ; 48 ; 53
13. Yes, each alien is 5 cm taller than the previous one.

14a.

Year	2002	2003	2004	2005	2006	2007
No. of Wax Figures	145	170	195	220	245	270

b. 295
c. 2010

15a.

Month	Jul	Aug	Sep	Oct	Nov	Dec
No. of Visitors	1800	2000	2300	2700	3200	3800

b. 4500
c. April

16. 10
17. 3
18. 5
19. 6
20. 8
21. 7
22. 6 + y = 11 ; 5
23. 2 x c = 8 ; 4
24. k – 8 = 20 ; 28
25. b ÷ 9 = 5 ; 45
26. 5 + m = 17 ; 12
27. g x 4 = 32 ; 8
28. u – 3 = 4 ; 7
29. a x 6 = 24 ; 4

Activity

1. (3 x y) cm
2. (y + 4) cm
3. (3 x y – 2) cm
4. Sister Worm

15 *Transformations and Coordinates*

1. 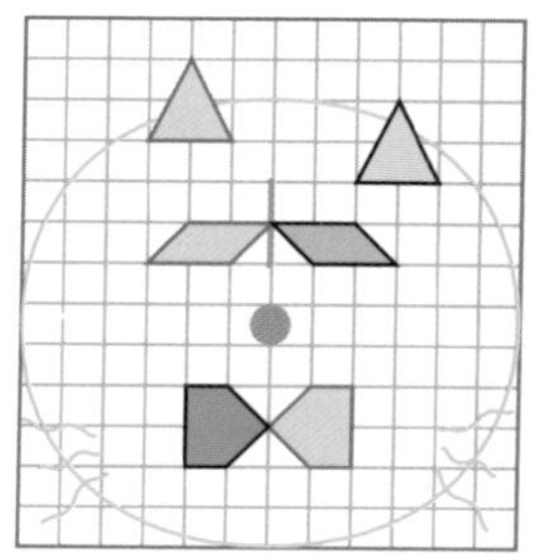

2. Yes
3. 2 square units
4. The coordinates are (4,4), (5,4), (6,3), (5,2), and (4,2).
5. 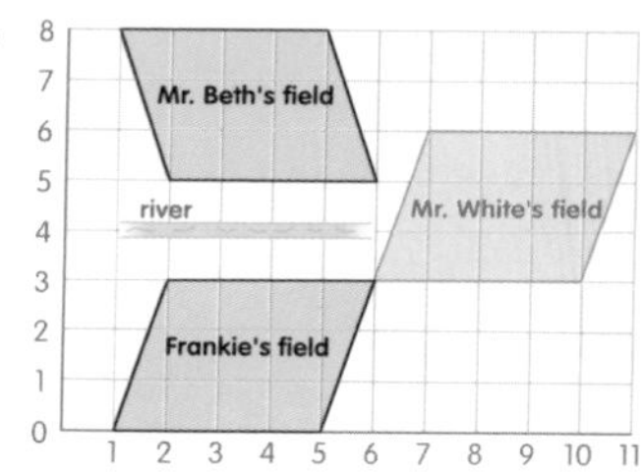

   ; (5,0)
6. 12
7. The coordinates are (1,8), (5,8), (6,5), and (2,5).
8. Rotation. Rotate Frankie's field $\frac{1}{2}$ turn about (6,3)./
   Translation. Translate Frankie's field 3 units up and 5 units right.

Activity

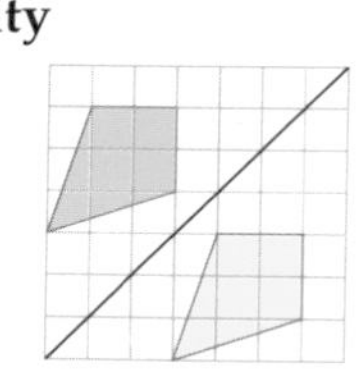

16 *Graphs and Probability*

1.

Colour	Green	Purple	Red
No. of Blocks	4	2	10
Fraction of the Whole	$\frac{1}{4}$	$\frac{1}{8}$	$\frac{5}{8}$

2. 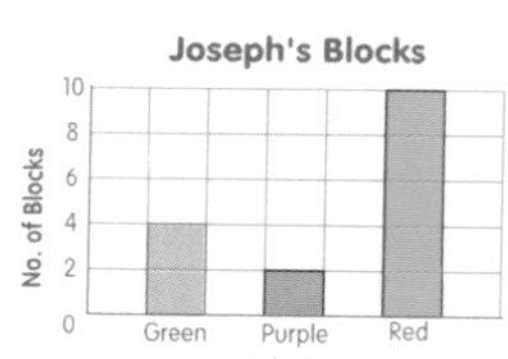

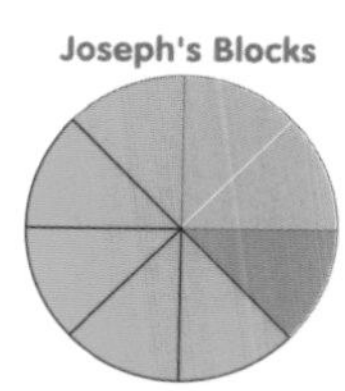

3. The circle graph
4. The bar graph
5.

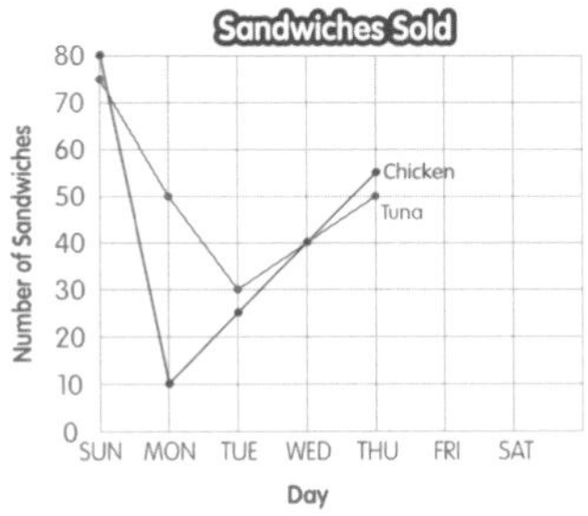

6. 49   7. 40
8. 50   9. 85 ; 70
10. 24 cups, 24 cups, 24 cups, 64 cups, 64 cups, 70 cups, 73 cups ; 49 cups ; 64 cups ; 24 cups
11. 15 bags, 15 bags, 15 bags, 18 bags, 18 bags, 21 bags ; 17 bags ; 16.5 bags ; 15 bags

12a. $\frac{1}{6}$ b. $\frac{1}{2}$ c. $\frac{1}{3}$

13.

14.

15.

16.

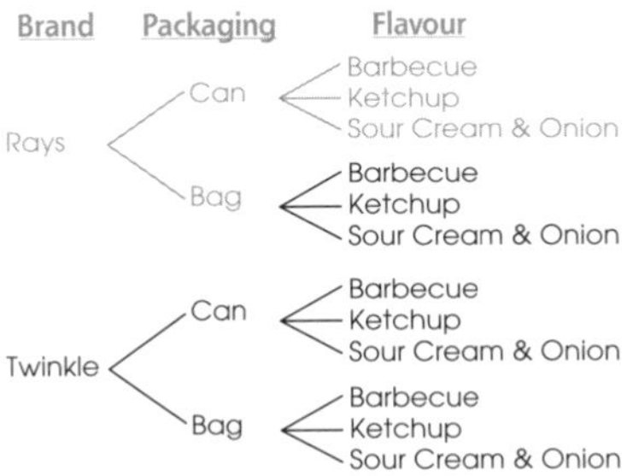

17. 12   18. 6
19. 4

20a. $\frac{4}{12}$ or $\frac{1}{3}$ b. $\frac{6}{12}$ or $\frac{1}{2}$

Activity

1. $\frac{3}{8}$ 2. $\frac{4}{16}$ or $\frac{1}{4}$

Final Test

1. 70%   2. 925%
3. 283%   4. 17%
5. 9.917   6. 2.236
7. 43.722   8. 0.998
9. 6.46   10. 47
11. 13.12
12. 720 cm^3 ; 290 cm^3 13. 128 m^3

14. 1:1   15. 1:2
16. 2:3   17. 2:1
18-21. (Suggested answers)
18. 6:14   19. 2:1
20. 9:12   21. 18:8
22.

23. $\frac{1}{4}$
24. $\frac{6}{9} = \frac{2}{3}$ 25. $\frac{6}{12} = \frac{1}{2}$
26. $\frac{4}{6} - \frac{1}{6} = \frac{3}{6} = \frac{1}{2}$ 27. $\frac{3}{10} + \frac{5}{10} = \frac{8}{10} = \frac{4}{5}$

28-30.

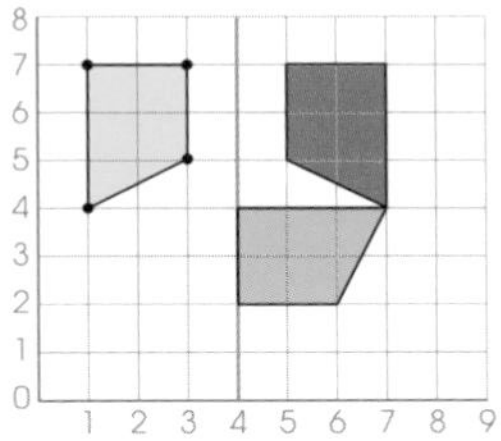

31. Yes
32. 3.41   33. 1.80
34. 3.12   35. 1.32
36. 3.22 m/s   37. 17.64 m
38. 32.22 m
39. A : 120 cm^2 B : 18 cm^2
40.

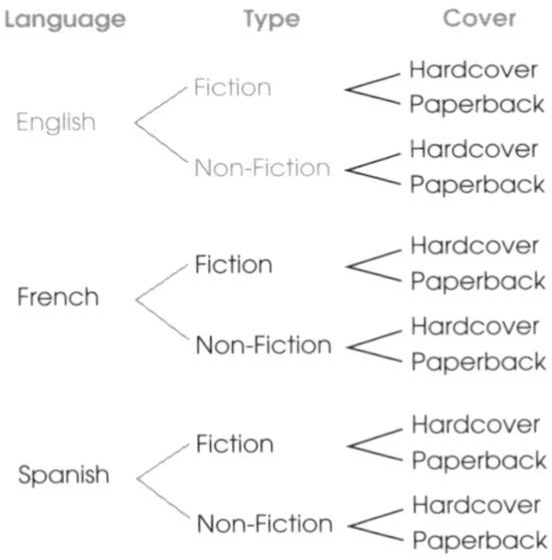

41. 12   42. 4
43a. $\frac{1}{12}$ b. $\frac{2}{12}$ or $\frac{1}{6}$ c. $\frac{6}{12}$ or $\frac{1}{2}$
44. $k \div 5 = 7$; The number is 35.
45. $p + 8 = 24$; The number is 16.
46a. 38.5 ; 46
b. 10:45 a.m.
c. 76 km

47. 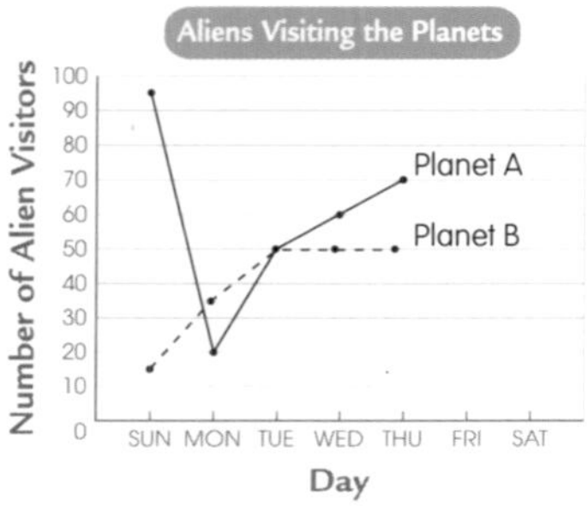

48. 59 aliens
49. 50 aliens
50. The number of aliens visiting Planet B increases gradually. Starting from Tuesday, the number of visitors is the same each day.
51a. 1005
b. 824
c. 206.5
52. 678.5
53. 824
54. Number of stars:Total number of shapes = 10:25 = 2:5
The ratio is 2:5.
55. $\frac{4}{5} + \frac{1}{2} = 1\frac{3}{10}$
She takes $1\frac{3}{10}$ h to cover the whole journey.
56. 4.08 ÷ 12 = 0.34
Amy needs to pay $0.34.

Assessment Test I

1. 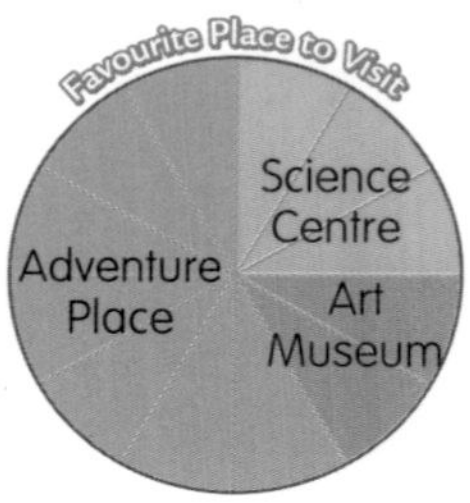

2. 2:5
(Number of boys:Number of girls = 4:10 = 2:5 ; 2:5 is the simplest form of 4:10.)
3. 13:11
(There are 13 girls and 11 boys in Mrs. Martin's class.)
4. She is correct, because there are 24 children in her class; 50% of 24 children is 12 children. There are 14 children who want to go to Adventure Place, which is more than 50% of the class.
5. For every 8 tickets, there is 1 free ticket.

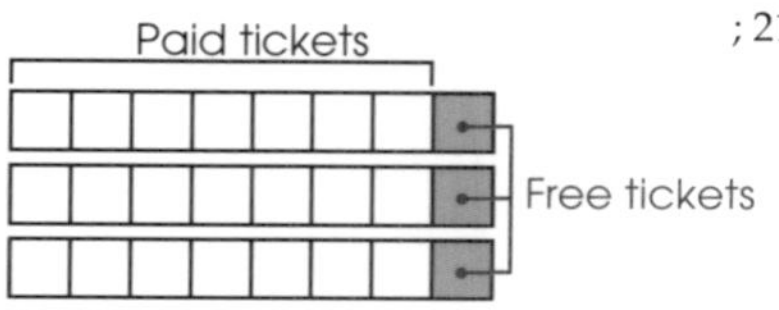

; 21

6. 494.55
(21 x $23.55 = $494.55)
7. There are 24 children. The children can be put into:
- 1 group with 24 children
- 2 groups with 12 children in each group
- 3 groups with 8 children in each group
- 4 groups with 6 children in each group

8. 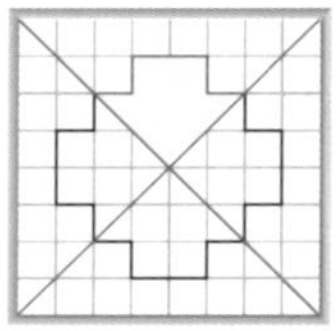
9. 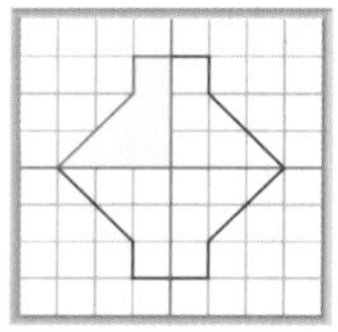

10. June 29
(The prime numbers between 24 and 34 are 29 and 31. There are only 30 days in June. Therefore, 29 is the answer.)
11. 17:00
(5 hours after noon is 5:00 p.m.)
12. 9 hours
(From 8:00 a.m. to 12:00 p.m., there are 4 hours. From 12:00 p.m. to 5:00 p.m., there are 5 hours. Therefore, there are 9 hours in all.)
13. (Suggested answer)

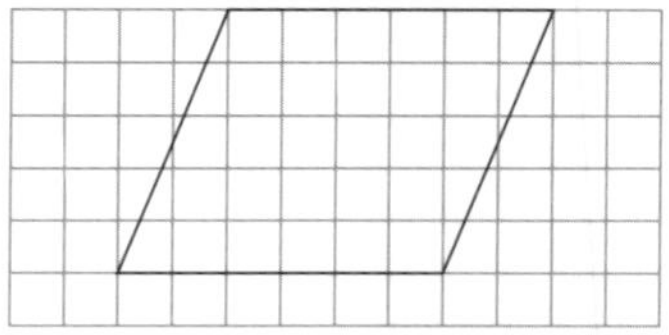

(The area of the parallelogram is 3000 cm². A parallelogram with base 60 cm and height 50 cm is one of the possible answers.)
14. A, D
(27 and 18 are multiples of 3.)
15. 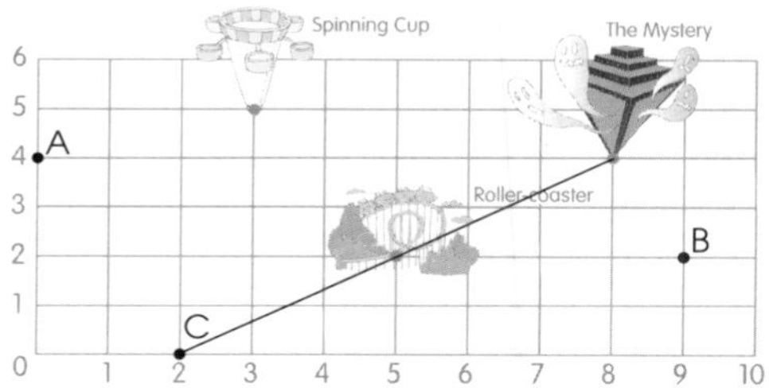

16a. (0,0)
b. (3,5)
c. (8,4)
d. (5,2)
17. 400 ; 0.4
(The distance between Ferris Wheel and Roller-coaster is the same as the distance between The Mystery and Roller-coaster. 400 m = (400 ÷ 1000) km = 0.4 km)
18. 52 min
(Use subtraction to find the answer.; 12:37 (regrouped as 11:97) − 11:45 = 52)
19. 13:58
(Use addition to find the answer. ; 13:35 + 23 = 13:58)
20. 14:55
(Use subtraction to find the answer. ; 15:05 (regrouped as 14:65) − 10 = 14:55)
21. 5:7 (There are 7 red cars.) ;
16 (1 min ⟶ 4 revolutions ; 4 min ⟶ 16 (4 x 4) revolutions)
22. 432 m³ (12 x 12 x 3 = 432) ;
588 m³ (14 x 14 x 3 = 588) ;
768 m³ (16 x 16 x 3 = 768) ;
972 m³ (18 x 18 x 3 = 972) ;
1200 m³ (20 x 20 x 3 = 1200) ;

40 (25 x 2 – 10) ;
70 (40 x 2 – 10) ;
130 (70 x 2 – 10)

23. 8
(The order of rotational symmetry is the number of times the figure can fit on itself in one complete rotation.)

24a. 3 b. 2
c. 5 d. 6
e. 4

25.

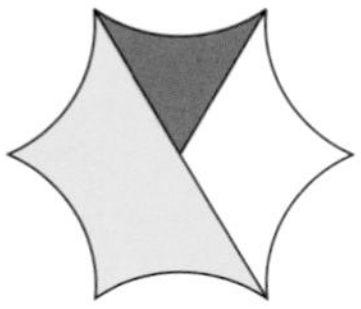

(Divide the shape into 6 equal parts. 1 part is green and 3 parts are yellow.)

26.

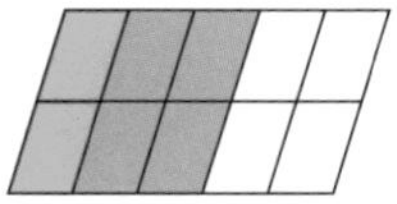

(0.2 = $\frac{2}{10}$; 40% = $\frac{4}{10}$; Divide the shape into 10 parts; 2 parts are orange and 4 parts are blue.)

27. m
28. 20 (Travels 40 km in 1 h; 20 km in $\frac{1}{2}$ h)
29. 24 (6 x 4 = 24)
30. 1:2
(There are 8 (24 – 16) adults on the train. The ratio is 8:16 = 1:2)
31. 2 ; 35
(Use subtraction to find the answer. ; $\begin{array}{r} {\scriptstyle 41\ \ 63} \\ 13:\not{4}\not{2}:\not{0}\not{3} \\ -\ 13:39:28 \\ \hline 2:35 \end{array}$)
32. 20
($\frac{4}{20} = \frac{20}{100}$ = 20%)
33. 21 ((24 + 19 + 24 + 23 + 21 + 15) ÷ 6 = 21) ;
24 ;
22 Put the data in order: (15, 19, 21, 23, 24, 24 ; Median: (21 + 23) ÷ 2 = 22)
34. A ; -5 ; 5 ; below
35. B, D
36.

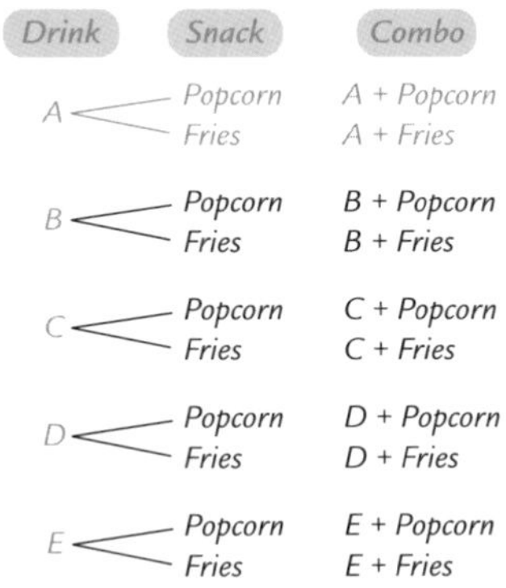

37. $\frac{5}{10}$ or $\frac{1}{2}$ 38. $\frac{2}{10}$ or $\frac{1}{5}$
39. $2.88 ($5.75 ÷ 2 = $2.875)

Assessment Test II

1.

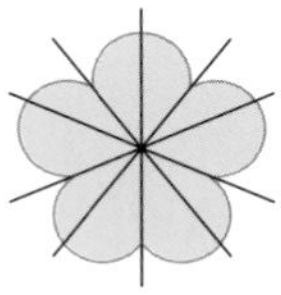

2. 5
3. 450 cm^2
(The length of the frame is 30 cm. The width of the frame is 15 cm (30 ÷ 2). The area of the frame is 450 cm^2 (30 x 15).)
4. Three million two hundred seventy-five thousand dollars
5. 3.25 tonnes (1000 kg = 1 t ; 3250 kg = 3.25 t)
6. 3:30 p.m.
7.

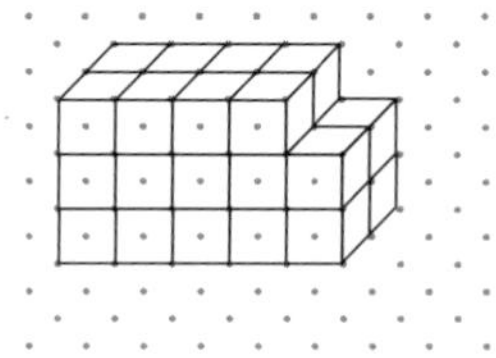

8.

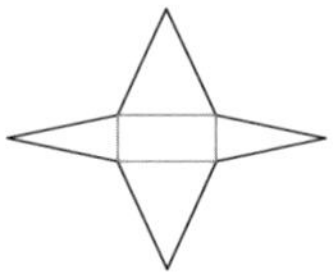

(A rectangular pyramid has 5 faces in all; 1 of them is rectangular and 4 are triangular.)

9.

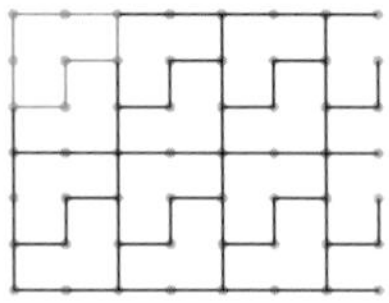 ; 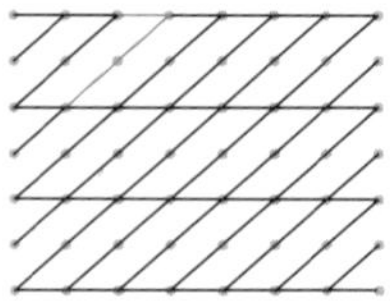

10. 7440 (16 x 465 = 7440)
11. $\frac{6}{10}$, 0.6, 60%
(6 out of 10 squares are coloured.)
12. $\frac{39}{100}$, 0.39, 39%
(39 out of 100 squares are coloured.)
13. 462 (10 329 – 9867 = 462)
14. 3 (15 ÷ 5 = 3)
15. 26 488 (43 x 28 x 22 = 26 488)
16. 6.25 (62.5 ÷ 10 = 6.25)
17. 28 (28 has 6 factors. They are 1, 2, 4, 7, 14, 28.)
18. (Suggested answer)

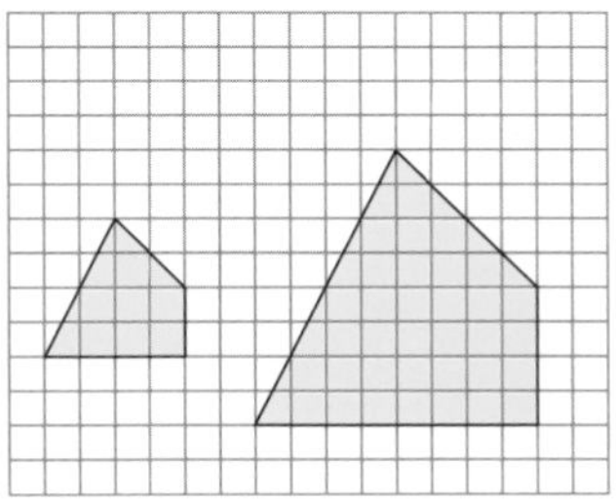

19. A : 500 (20 x 25 = 500)
B : 216 (24 x 18 ÷ 2 = 216)

20. 84%

21. 32% (16 cookies (50 – 34) are left.)

22. 6 min 9 s

(Use subtraction to find the answer. ; $\begin{array}{r} 13:11:25 \\ -\ 13:05:16 \\ \hline 6:09 \end{array}$)

23. 126.35 mL (250 – 123.65 = 126.35)

24.

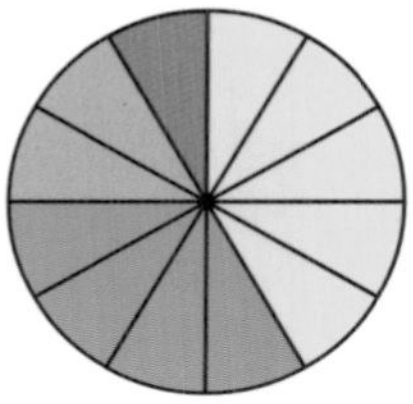

25a. $\frac{1}{12}$

b. $\frac{9}{12}$ or $\frac{3}{4}$

c. 0

d. $\frac{10}{12}$ or $\frac{5}{6}$

26. The distance travelled is 10.37 km (2.93 + 3.88 + 3.56). The places that Gary's father passes by are Parkway Inn and Skyline City.

27. 28 min

(Use subtraction to find the answer. ; $\begin{array}{r} 14:36 \\ -\ 14:08 \\ \hline 28 \end{array}$)

28. $89.25

(Find out how much the worker earns in 1 hour first. Earnings: $107.10 ÷ 6 = $17.85. Then use multiplication to find the answer. Earnings in 5 hours: 5 x $17.85 = $89.25)

29. $7\frac{1}{3}$ hours

(Total number of hours: $3\frac{7}{12} + 3\frac{3}{4} = 3\frac{7}{12} + 3\frac{9}{12}$

$= 6\frac{16}{12} = 7\frac{4}{12} = 7\frac{1}{3}$)

30. 10 000

31. 3 months

(The months are February, August, and September.)

32. $35 000

(Write the profits in order from least to greatest: ($20 000, $20 000, $30 000, $30 000, $35 000, $40 000, $50 000, $50 000, $60 000) The number in the middle is the median.)

33. $90 000

(

Aug	Sep	Oct	Nov	Dec
50 000	60 000	70 000	80 000	90 000

+ 10 000 + 10 000 + 10 000 + 10 000)

34. 2:5

(Profit made in May:Profit made in Feb = 20 000:50 000 = 2:5)

35. 28 min

(Use subtraction to find the answer. ; $\begin{array}{r} \overset{20}{\cancel{21}}:\overset{63}{\cancel{03}} \\ -\ 20:35 \\ \hline 28 \end{array}$)

36. 12.5 words/min (Writing 350 words in 28 min. ; Rate: 350 ÷ 28 = 12.5)

the SMURFS™

Welcome, Baby Smurf!

by Peyo

SIMON SPOTLIGHT
New York London Toronto Sydney New Delhi
An imprint of Simon & Schuster Children's Publishing Division
1230 Avenue of the Americas, New York, New York 10020

Originally published in French in 2008 as *Le Bébé Schtroumpf* written by Peyo

For information about special discounts for bulk purchases, please contact Simon & Schuster Special Sales at 1-866-506-1949 or business@simonandschuster.com.
Manufactured in the United States of America 1213 LAK
First Edition 2 4 6 8 10 9 7 5 3 1
ISBN 978-1-4424-9542-5

On the night of a full moon, when all the Smurfs were sleeping soundly in their homes, a stork arrived in Smurf Village. The stork was carrying a big bundle in her beak, and after a gentle landing, she set the bundle down in front of a Smurf's house.

She tapped on the door a few times with her beak, and then, when she was sure she had woken up the Smurf who lived there, she flew off and left the package behind to be discovered.

Lazy Smurf was not very happy to be woken up in the middle of the night. Half asleep, he opened his door and discovered the package waiting for him . . . a baby Smurf in a basket!

"What am I going to smurf with this baby?" Lazy asked.

He decided to take the baby to Smurfette.

Smurfette was very happy when she saw the baby. She took him in her arms and brought him inside to warm him up and to feed him. Lazy Smurf was relieved that he chose to bring the baby to Smurfette.

The next day, word spread through Smurf Village about the new baby Smurf. The Smurfs were very excited about the new arrival . . . every Smurf except Grouchy, who is never excited about *anything*.

"I don't like Baby Smurf!" Grouchy complained. He couldn't understand why everyone was fussing so much over the little baby.

But Grouchy was the only Smurf who felt that way. The other Smurfs loved the new baby and worked together to make sure he was safe and happy. When it was time to take the baby for a walk in his stroller, Smurfette had more volunteers than she needed to help out!

Meanwhile, Brainy Smurf couldn't help but wonder where the baby Smurf came from. He decided to go ask Papa Smurf.

Papa Smurf admitted that he did not know why Baby Smurf appeared in their village. “It is a great mystery,” Papa Smurf explained. “But mysteries are a part of life, so we should just enjoy our new baby Smurf!”

Brainy loved the little baby too . . . but he still wondered *why* the baby arrived. *There must be a logical explanation*, he thought.

Brainy Smurf was right; there was an explanation. The next day the stork returned to Smurf Village, carrying a letter in her beak. She gave it to Papa Smurf, and as the other Smurfs gathered around, he read it out loud.

"'Dear Smurfs,'" read Papa. "'Due to an error in our shipping department, you received a baby who was not meant for you. Please send him back to us. Thank you very much.'"

Papa Smurf could barely finish reading over the shouts and cries of all the Smurfs. “How can we return our beloved Baby Smurf?” the Smurfs all asked.

The stork felt very bad.

“We don’t blame you,” Papa Smurf told the sad stork. “We know you’re just doing your job.”

Smurfette ran off to get Baby Smurf but then returned a moment later waving her arms and shouting.

"Baby Smurf has disappeared!" she yelled. "He's gone!"

The Smurfs were confused. They knew that Baby Smurf could not have left on his own because he was just a baby. . . . He couldn't even walk yet.

"Grouchy has disappeared as well!" Hefty Smurf realized.

The Smurfs split up to search for Baby Smurf and Grouchy.
They walked through the woods calling, “Baby! Grouchy! Where are you?”

Some rabbits heard them and came out to see what all the commotion was about.

The rabbits weren't the only ones who heard the Smurfs. . . .

The evil wizard Gargamel also heard them! "This time I've got you!" he yelled as he jumped from behind a bush and tried to grab Hefty.

But Hefty was so worried about Baby Smurf that he wasn't afraid of Gargamel! "Oh, smurf me alone!" he told Gargamel as he escaped. "I don't have time to smurf with you! I have to find Baby Smurf!"

Gargamel was so shocked that he fell down on the ground, kicking and screaming. "This is unbelievable!" he yelled to his cat, Azrael.

Before long, it was nighttime and a storm was coming, so Papa Smurf called off the search.

The Smurfs were very sad and did not want to stop searching, but they knew it was not safe outside anymore. Back in Smurf Village, Smurfette cried because she missed Baby Smurf so much . . . and because she was so worried about Baby and Grouchy.

And speaking of Grouchy . . . he had been hiding deep in the woods with Baby Smurf. When he heard that the stork was going to take the baby away, Grouchy ran off to hide him until the stork left. But it wasn't safe to be outside in the storm, and Grouchy knew he had to take the baby back to Smurf Village. It was the right thing to do.

When Grouchy Smurf returned to Smurf Village, Smurfette heard Baby Smurf's cries and ran to meet them. Grouchy promised not to run off again.

"I'm just glad Baby Smurf is home!" she shouted happily.

"But not for long," said Papa Smurf. "We must smurf the right thing and give him back to the stork. He is not meant to be ours."

The stork arrived at Smurf Village once again, this time to pick up the baby. The Smurfs were sad to say good-bye to their beloved Baby Smurf, but Grouchy was the saddest Smurf of all. They all cried as the stork flew off.

It had been a long, sad day, and the Smurfs went to sleep. The weather had improved, but none of that mattered to the Smurfs anymore.

But then the next morning, they woke up to hear a very familiar sound . . .

. . . the sound of the stork's wings flapping! She had returned to Smurf Village with Baby Smurf and a note! It had wonderful news: Because the Smurfs loved the baby so much, it had been decided that they could keep him forever. The Smurfs were so happy that they decided to throw a party.

"I don't like parties!" grumbled Grouchy.

But deep down, he was secretly very happy that everything worked out so perfectly!